Mies van der Rohe

MIES VAN DER ROHE

by Philip C. Johnson

THE MUSEUM OF MODERN ART, NEW YORK

Distributed by New York Graphic Society, Boston

Third edition, revised: copyright © 1978 by The Museum of Modern Art

Second edition, revised: copyright © 1953

First edition: copyright © 1947, renewed 1975

All rights reserved

Library of Congress Catalog Card Number 77-90996

ISBN 0-87070-560-1

The Museum of Modern Art

11 West 53 Street, New York, N.Y. 10019

Printed in the United States of America

CONTENTS

ACKNOWLEDGMENTS

I wish to thank above all Professor Mies van der Rohe for his close collaboration in every part of the work: assembling material, making special drawings, selecting illustrations and designing the jacket of the book. Special thanks are also due to Jon Stroup for his thorough editing; George Danforth, for drawing plans, securing photographs and collaborating on the bibliography; Hannah B. Muller, for the bibliography as well as invaluable research assistance in locating rare items; Carlus Dyer, the typographer of this volume; Martin James, for his help with translations from the German; Lilly Reich, for assembling European material; J. B. Neumann, who first introduced me to Mies, in 1930, for the portrait of Mies.

For special information and photographs: Pierre Blouke, Meric Callery, Howard Dearstyne, Petro van Doesburg, Ludwig Hilberseimer, Frederick Kiesler, K. Lönberg-Holm, Sybil Moholy-Nagy, Hugo Perls, Hans Richter and James Speyer.

For advice and criticism of the text: Alfred H. Barr, Jr., Henry-Russell Hitchcock, Edgar Kaufmann, Jr.; for their general assistance: Ruth Lowe Bookman and Ada Louise Huxtable of the Department of Architecture.

On behalf of the Museum I wish to thank most especially the following for their generous contributions which made possible the size and scope of the book and exhibition: David Pleydell Bouverie, Joseph Cantor, Philip L. Goodwin, Edgar Kaufmann, Jr., Mrs. Stanley B. Resor.

P. C. J.

PREFACE TO THE FIRST EDITION

Of all the great modern architects Mies van der Rohe is the least known. Although his outstanding buildings, such as the Barcelona Pavilion and the Tugendhat house, have been illustrated in the magazines of many countries, no monograph treating his work as a whole has yet been published. Only two articles devoted exclusively to Mies have appeared: one by Paul Westheim published twenty years ago (bibl. 82) and one by myself fifteen years ago (bibl. 53), both of which are now out of date.

All the buildings and projects which Mies considers in any way important are illustrated in this volume, with the exception of a few buildings which were not executed according to his standards and some projects of the 1910-1914 period which were destroyed in the bombing of Berlin. In addition, all of Mies's writings, published or unpublished, are included with the exception of a few items considered repetitious or too topical to be of lasting interest.

This monograph is published on the occasion of an exhibition of the architecture of Mies van der Rohe held at the Museum of Modern Art, September 16–November 23, 1947.

NOTE TO THE THIRD EDITION

Philip Johnson's *Mies van der Rohe* was first published in 1947; a second edition, revised and enlarged, was issued in 1953. The present publication reproduces the text of the 1953 edition, unaltered except for corrections in the dating of several early projects. The additions include an Epilogue, in the form of an interview, in which Mr. Johnson discusses aspects of Mies's personality and work. The Chronology and the List of Works have been extended to cover Mies's full career; in the List of Works, the major structures erected after 1953 are illustrated. A supplemental note has been added to the Bibliography.

Ludwig Glaeser
Curator, Mies van der Rohe Archive
The Museum of Modern Art

1886 – 1919

Ludwig Mies—he later added his mother's surname, van der Rohe—was born in 1886 in the ancient city of Aachen (Aix-la-Chapelle) on the border of Germany and the Low Countries. Aachen, the first capital of the Holy Roman Empire, had been the center of Western culture during the Early Middle Ages, and the Cathedral School, which Mies attended, had been founded by Charlemagne in the ninth century. He has ever since been conscious of his heritage; the medieval concept of order expressed in the writings of St. Augustine and St. Thomas Aquinas has influenced his architectural philosophy fully as much as modern principles of functionalism and structural clarity.

Mies van der Rohe never received any formal architectural training. He learned the first lesson of building—the placing of stone on stone—from his father, a master mason and the proprietor of a small stone cutting shop. By actually working with stone he acquired as a boy what many school-trained architects never learn—a thorough knowledge of the possibilities and limitations of masonry construction—and as a result of his early training he has never been guilty of the solecisms of "paper architecture."

When he was fifteen he left the trade school which he had attended for two years to work first as an apprentice and then as a draftsman for local designers and architects. He became adept at freehand delineation through his training as a designer of the "Renaissance" stucco decorations that festooned the speculative buildings of the period. He now describes this apprenticeship as grueling, but it developed his talent for drawing which later enabled him to produce the most beautiful architectural renderings of the present century.

In 1905, at the age of nineteen, Mies went to Berlin, where he was employed by an architect designing in wood. Soon dissatisfied with his inadequate knowledge of the material, he apprenticed himself to Bruno

Paul, the leading furniture and cabinet designer of Germany. Two years later he left Paul's office to build his first house as an independent architect.

Mies considers the Riehl house too uncharacteristic to publish, but according to a contemporary critic, "the work is so faultless that no one would guess that it is the first independent work of a young architect" (bibl. 17). Designed in the then popular traditional eighteenth-century style with steep roofs, gables and dormer windows, it was distinguishable from its contemporaries only by fine proportions and careful execution.

In 1907 the eighteenth-century manner was the fashionable style in Germany, as it had been for the preceding fifty years and continued to be until World War II. But in opposition to the dictates of fashion stood a few architects like Peter Behrens (1868-1938), soon to become Mies's teacher, who were reinterpreting the Neo-Classic tradition, and a very small group led by the intransigent Belgian architect, Henry van de Velde (born 1863), who were still working in the modern manner of the nineties.

This modernism was a blend of the English Arts and Crafts Movement, which combined picturesqueness with a nascent functionalism, and the *Art Nouveau,* a decorative manner characterized by curvilinear forms. It reached its culmination in the Darmstadt Exposition of 1901. Intended to evoke a renascence of all the arts under the leadership of architecture, the Exposition consisted of a group of permanent buildings and houses designed by the brilliant Austrian architect, Joseph Maria Olbrich(1867-1908), and Peter Behrens. The latter, who had been solely a craftsman and designer until then, built his first house there—a tall, awkward box crowned with exotic ogival gables. It was to be his only house in the modern manner. Within four years a general reaction to modernism had set in, and his pavilion for Oldenburg was a design composed of clear Neo-Classic cubes. Like many of his contemporaries, he was seeking what the modernism of the nineties so conspicuously lacked: order and integration.

Behrens was fast becoming the leading progressive architect of Germany. Beginning in 1906, as architect for the electrical industry, the AEG,

Peter Behrens: Turbine Factory, Berlin. 1909

he built a series of factories and office buildings in which for the first time since the Industrial Revolution architectural forms were based on engineering. Though the development of steel and glass as building materials had begun in the early nineteenth century, architects, intent on emulating past styles, had been unable to exploit their potentialities. Engineering and architecture had been divorced. The AEG buildings, of which the steel and glass turbine factory (above) is the best example, signalized their reunion. However, although Behrens could bring about this fusion in his industrial work, the time was not ripe for its universal acceptance. In his domestic and monumental buildings he continued to achieve simplicity and order through his personal interpretation of the Neo-Classic tradition.

Behrens' office became a training ground for the modern architects of the next generation. Walter Gropius (born 1883), who later organized the Bauhaus in Weimar, was one of his chief designers; Le Corbusier (born 1887), who was to become France's leading architect, served a brief apprenticeship; and in 1908, Mies van der Rohe, after finishing the Riehl house, came to work for the famous architect as a draftsman and designer.

During the following three years—the most decisive of his early career—Mies acquired a wealth of practical experience, especially as supervisor of construction for the German Embassy at St. Petersburg. Most important, he absorbed the respect for detail which Behrens as an industrial designer could give him, and an appreciation of order through his study of Neo-Classic architecture. Although he must have observed the structural honesty of the turbine factory, its direct influence on his work cannot be seen until the early twenties when he was experimenting with the design of steel and glass skyscrapers (pages 23-29). More immediate was the influence on his work of Neo-Classicism, which Behrens had derived from the work of the German architect, Schinkel.

Peter Behrens: Schröder house, Hagen-Eppenhausen, Germany. 1911

Perls house, Berlin-Zehlendorf. 1911

Karl Friedrich Schinkel: project for a casino, Potsdam, Germany. c. 1836

Karl Friedrich Schinkel (1781-1840) was the greatest architect of the Romantic period in Europe. Until the recent destruction of Berlin, his buildings, especially the Altes Museum and the Staatstheater, were landmarks in a city otherwise devoid of fine architecture. Most of his work was "Greek," but he built many fine "Gothic" churches and "Italian" palaces, and designed a department store in no particular style featuring large areas of glass. His greatness, however, lay in his unique sense of proportion, which transformed whatever style he used.

Schinkel's influence on Mies van der Rohe is first seen in the house the young architect built for Hugo Perls in 1911 (page 13). Mies built this house while he was working for Behrens, and although it is similar in style to his teacher's Schinkelesque house of the same year for the Schröders (page 12), it is even closer to the spirit of the great Romantic. The countersunk portico, the deep cornice and the low-pitched roof are all Schinkel motifs. This house is not the work of a student; Mies at the age of twenty-five had become as accomplished a designer in the Schinkel tradition as his teacher.

As Behrens' apprentice, Mies helped design a house for Mme

Project: Kröller house, The Hague, Holland. 1912

Kröller house: full scale wood and canvas model erected on actual site

15

H. E. L. J. Kröller, the owner of the famous Kröller-Müller collection of modern painting. After he left Behrens' office, Mme Kröller invited him to The Hague, where he lived for a year designing his own version of the house (page 15) and eventually constructing a full-scale mock-up in wood and canvas (page 15). During this year, he also entered a competition for the Bismarck Monument (opposite).

Both projects are Schinkelesque. In the monument, the romantic site and the free use of traditional elements are particularly reminiscent; while the dominating stone pier is an original motif that Mies has since used in his domestic buildings (pages 32, 78). The Schinkelesque features of the Kröller house become evident when it is compared to Schinkel's own design for a casino (page 14). A number of features in each building are remarkably alike: the pyramidal massing, the proportioning of the colonnades, the method of joining wing to main block and colonnade to wing, as well as the decorative details. Despite these similarities, however, there is no pedantic revivalism in Mies's reference to Schinkel's designs. Unlike many of his contemporaries, he never used Schinkel as a quarry for architectural clichés. It is almost as if he had been one of that band of Schinkel followers—alliteratively called *Schinkelschüler*—who emulated him during his life and immediately after his death. But Mies did not hesitate to break with precedent in order to meet the requirements of his own age. For instance, in the Kröller house he used many more windows than were justified by the Schinkel tradition, yet he managed to incorporate them without destroying the Romantic massing of the building.

While in The Hague, Mies was impressed by the buildings of the Dutch architect, Hendrik Petrus Berlage (1859-1934) who, with Behrens, was an important forerunner of modern architecture. Behrens approached architecture from the point of view of form, Berlage from the point of view of structure. Thus the former contributed the reduction of Neo-Classic shapes to simple rectangular blocks, the latter, the practice of structural honesty derived from the theories of Ruskin and Morris: namely, that those parts of a building resembling supports should actually support and, conversely, that all the supporting elements should be evident.

Project: Bismarck Monument, Bingen on the Rhine, Germany. 1912

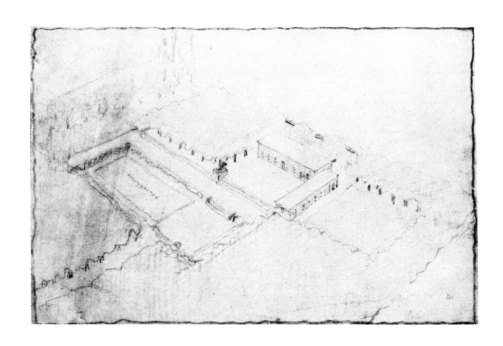

Urbig house, Berlin-Neubabelsberg. 1914

opposite: **Projects: two versions of a house for the architect, Werder, Germany. 1914**

Project: Kempner house, Berlin. 1919

Berlage also inherited from Ruskin his hatred of the Renaissance, with its useless pilasters, but whereas Ruskin advocated a revival of the Gothic, Berlage emphasized honest contemporary building rather than a return to any particular style. At the same time, in emulating the craftsmen of the Middle Ages, whom he greatly admired, he brought to his own work a vaguely medieval character. It was not, however, Berlage's forms that influenced the young Mies, but his integrity, especially in the use of the typical Lowlands material, brick.

The Kröller house was never built and in 1913, after completing the designs, Mies returned to Berlin and opened his own architectural office. Shortly afterwards he designed two versions of a house for himself at Werder (page 18), in which the formal aspect of the Schinkel tradition is emphasized. In the same year he proposed a Schinkelesque house for the Urbig family which they discarded, requesting instead an eighteenth-century villa (page 19). Even in this popular style, Mies maintained a classic serenity in contrast to the monumental fussiness generally achieved by his contemporaries.

When he returned from the war in 1919, he projected a house for the Kempner family (above), in which the flat roof, the triple arcade and the wide spacing of the tall, narrow windows closely resemble the Italianate work of Schinkel and the *Schinkelschüler*. This was Mies's last Romantic design.

20

1919–1925

In the first few years after the war, Mies van der Rohe published a series of projects so remarkable and so different from one another that it seems as if he were trying each year to invent a new kind of architecture. Out of the refined *Schinkelschüler* had developed a radical innovator. This personal revolution was symptomatic of the artistic ferment in Berlin, which had become the most feverishly active art center in post-war Europe.

During the war the development of German painting had been suspended and the capital, isolated from events abroad, had become an artistic and intellectual vacuum. Meanwhile, *de Stijl* had developed in Holland, Constructivism and Suprematism in Russia and Dadaism in Zurich. Unsealed by the Armistice, the liberated city sucked in these new movements, while German Expressionism, formerly most conspicuous in painting, gained a new impetus and exerted its influence in other fields, among them architecture.

Never in its history had architecture been so influenced by painting. Beginning in 1919, the "dislocated angles and distorted curves" of Expressionism (bibl. 67a) became the basis of a procession of fantastic projects, very few of which were ever built. In 1922 the founder of *de Stijl,* Theo van Doesburg, visited Berlin; and from Moscow came El Lissitzky to help organize the exhibition of Russian Constructivism and Suprematism. Soon afterwards the piling of interlocking cubical volumes and the overlapping of rectangular planes characteristic of these two movements could be seen in *avant-garde* projects. Unlike Expressionism, which petered out in the twenties, both *de Stijl* and Constructivism were to be assimilated by what has since become known as "modern architecture."

Painting as an influence was rivaled by technolatry, which swept over post-war Europe proclaiming the machine as the *deus ex machina* of the plastic arts. In Germany, as elsewhere, architects stripped their buildings of superfluous detail and made their surfaces smooth and plain; they exploited the esthetic effects of machine-made materials such as steel and glass; and like Le Corbusier, they began to think of their houses as "machines for living." Curiously enough, in re-examining the function of architecture they were extending the nineteenth-century philosophy of structural honesty, which had led its advocates to denounce the machine in favor of handicraft and Gothic revivalism.

Mies's activities in these days were manifold. Besides designing the remarkable series of projects which were to make him famous, he organized exhibitions, wrote articles and financed the magazine G, named for the initial letter of *Gestaltung* (creative force). Hans Richter, the abstract film artist and a member of *de Stijl,* was the publisher. Consequently, the magazine, which dealt with contemporary esthetic problems, had a strong *Stijl* flavor, although it carried articles by the Russian, El Lissitzky and by the Dadaists, George Grosz and Tristan Tzara, as well as scientific treatises on technology and the art of the insane.

Only the first three issues of G (1923–24) were financed by Mies, whose main activity during the post-war years was his work with the *Novembergruppe,* an organization named after the month of the Republican Revolution and founded to propagandize modern art. From its inception in 1918, this group held a series of annual exhibitions which became rallying points for progressive artists in all fields. Because architecture was believed to be the most social of the arts, it played an important part in the program. Mies, who headed the architectural section from 1921 until 1925, directed four exhibitions, in which four of his five most daring projects (pages 23–33) were included.

These five projects have been of seminal importance in the history of modern architecture. In them Mies van der Rohe rose above the influence of contemporary movements to an uncompromising directness of expression that has not yet been surpassed. Each design is the crystallization of a single unadulterated concept which, though shocking when it appeared, has since become part of the modern architect's stock in trade.

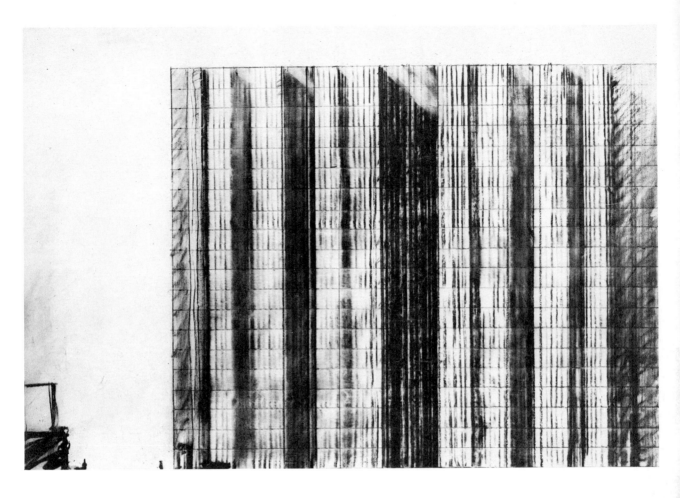

Project: office building, Friedrichstrasse, Berlin. 1921. First scheme

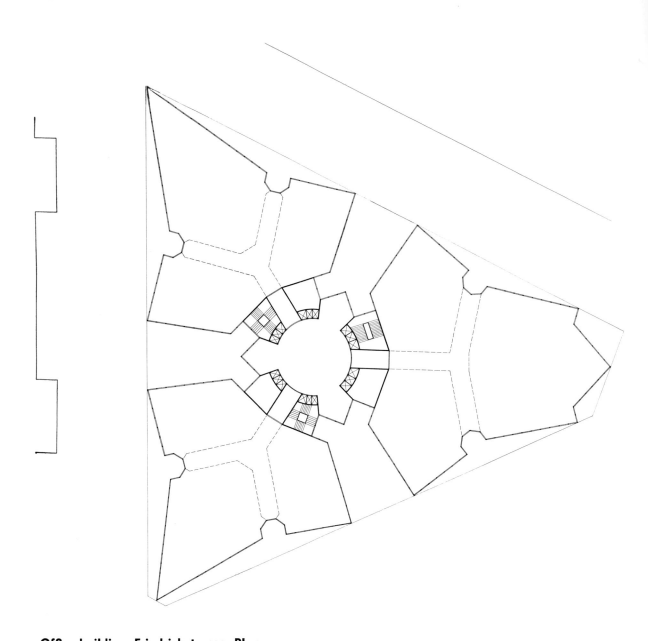

Office building, Friedrichstrasse. Plan

Project: office building, Friedrichstrasse, Berlin. 1921. First scheme

The first two projects were designs for glass skyscrapers: one in 1921 for the Friedrichstrasse in Berlin (pages 23–25), the other in 1922 for an ideal site (pages 27–29). These buildings, which Mies discusses in his article *Two Glass Skyscrapers* (page 187), mark the first proposed use of glass as the exterior surface of an office building. Heretofore, the extensive use of this material had been restricted to exposition buildings and a few department stores.

Mies's uncompromising directness is obvious in the renderings. No building could be more "glass" than these. Their glass walls rise uninterrupted to the top where, unadorned by cornices, they stop as though cut by shears. In addition, both projects have been designed to exploit the reflective qualities of the medium. The prismatic plan of the first is rather Expressionistic in its oblique angles, whereas the second plan has a free curvilinear form of astonishing originality. This form bears some resemblance to certain abstract film designs of Viking Eggeling and to the biomorphic shapes of the painter Jean (Hans) Arp; according to Mies, however, it evolved from a study of the play of light on a model hung outside his office window. Such a "free form" is unique in his work and did not appear in the work of other architects until the late thirties, when it was used only as a decorative motif.

The playful inventiveness of the skyscrapers is completely suppressed in the next project, the dry and elegant office building of 1922 (page 31). Here the entire design is based on a rigid structural system. Each floor slab is cantilevered from regularly spaced columns and turned up at the periphery to form parapet walls. The alternation of these walls with bands of ribbon windows constitutes the exterior elevations. Nothing more has been added in the way of decoration, and the building's extraordinary beauty derives solely from the proportioning of these structural and functional elements, exemplified in the subtle thinning of the two top bands. The solution of the entrance problem is natural and convincing. By merely interrupting the dominant horizontal on the ground floor, a dramatic effect is simply achieved and then intensified by the insertion of a broad, low flight of steps.

This project is the apotheosis of the ribbon window. Every advantage is taken of its horizontal nature; even the entrance break, rather than

Project: glass skyscraper. 1922

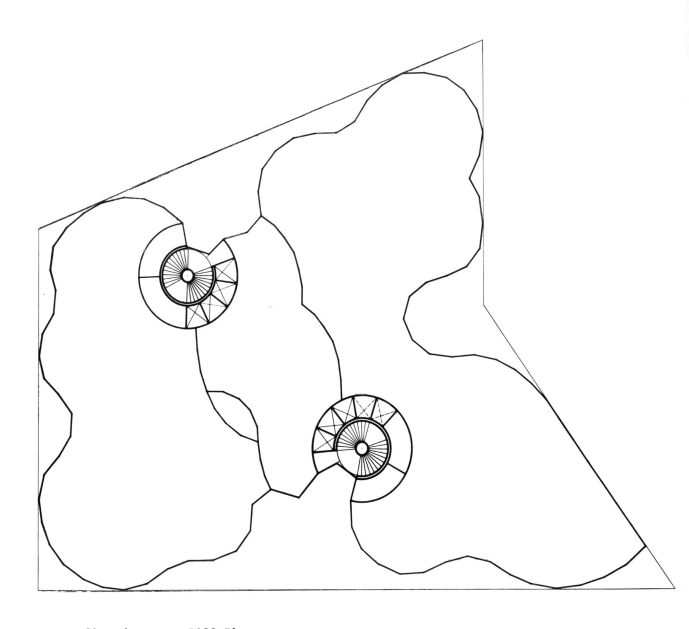

Glass skyscraper. 1922. Plan

Project: glass skyscraper. 1922. Model

detracting, serves as an accentuation. Although the ribbon window has become practically a cliché by now, no other architect has yet had the courage to use it so purely.

Mies described the structural system responsible for this purity in the first issue of G; he called it "skin and bones construction" (page 188), a description which led Theo van Doesburg to label him an "anatomical architect." Van Doesburg, as leader of de Stijl, was annoyed by Mies's severity just as the latter was annoyed by the formalistic interlocking cubes of de Stijl architecture. Yet it is amusing to note that in spite of these disagreements Mies, in working out his next project, a country house (page 32), arrived at a plan closely resembling the orthogonal patterns of a van Doesburg painting.

Again the design as a whole is remarkably original. Although Frank Lloyd Wright preceded him in breaking down the traditional idea of the house as a box with holes punched in it, Mies's approach is entirely his own. It depends upon a new conception of the function of the wall. The unit of design is no longer the cubic room but the free-standing wall, which breaks the traditional box by sliding out from beneath the roof and extending into the landscape. Instead of forming a closed volume, these independent walls, joined only by panes of glass, create a new ambiguous sensation of space. Indoors and outdoors are no longer easily defined; they flow into each other. This concept of an architecture of flowing space, channeled by free-standing planes, plays an important rôle in Mies's later development and reaches its supreme expression in the Barcelona Pavilion of 1929 (pages 66–74).

The last of the five projects, the country house of 1923 (page 33), is another and completely different solution of the breaking up of the box. It is also an investigation into the potentialities of reinforced concrete for domestic building. Here the box is not indiscriminately sliced by a profusion of independent walls, but carefully divided and pulled apart. The different areas, i.e. living area, sleeping area and service area, are isolated from each other in an admirably balanced swastika-like plan that combines the maximum of indoor and outdoor privacy with the minimum dispersal of architectural units. This is the first of the "zoned" houses of which we hear so much today.

Project: concrete office building. 1922

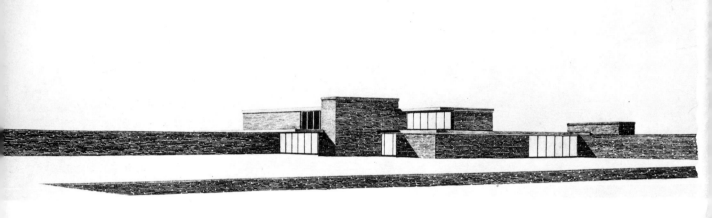

Project: brick country house. 1922

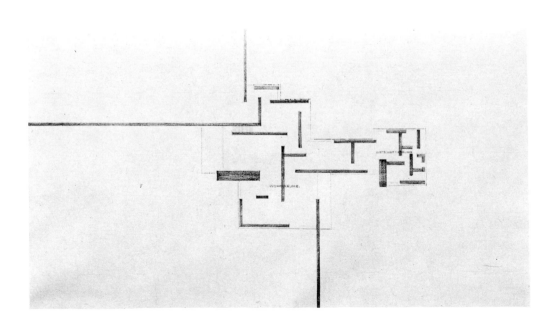

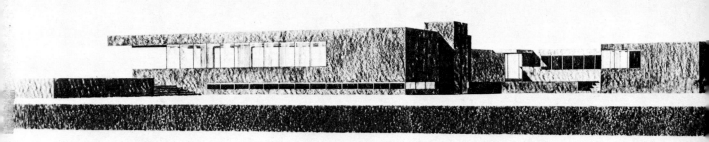

Project: concrete country house. 1923

Mies's position as a pioneer rests on these five projects. In the Europe of the twenties they were frequently published—so frequently, in fact, that he gained the reputation of being a visionary rather than a practical architect. Nothing could be further from the truth; Mies is first and foremost a builder, and these, unlike many of the projects designed by contemporaries during this period of scant construction, are technically buildable.

Their influence was due to at least two factors: the dazzling clarity of the designs and the beautiful manner in which they were presented. Mies's renderings, plans and photomontages are always pleasing in themselves. His plans, though regarded by him as mere hieroglyphs of his structures, are always satisfactory two-dimensional designs, and his drawings, particularly his charcoal study of the first glass skyscraper (page 23), are often works of art of excellent quality.

Modern architecture evolved during the years 1919 to 1924 when these five projects appeared. Besides Mies van der Rohe, three other men contributed significantly to its rapid development: Walter Gropius, J.J.P. Oud and Le Corbusier. Gropius, in Germany, had built his proto-modern Fagus factory with its clean lines and rational use of glass and brick as early as 1912, and in 1926 he designed the Bauhaus at Dessau, although during the immediate post-war period he stuck closely to the popular Expressionist and *Stijl* mannerisms. Oud, as city architect of Rotterdam, emerged from the influence of *de Stijl* by 1924 to design his subtly refined workers' houses in the Hook of Holland. And Le Corbusier, who by 1914 had already begun to think of design in terms of skeleton construction, raised his *prisme pur* off the ground in the Citrohan house of 1922.

But none of these men equalled the breadth or depth of Mies van der Rohe's pioneer work; none of them explored so far in so many different directions. Today Mies's projects seem least dated. His concrete office building of 1922 (page 31), if it were to be erected now, might strike us as rather extreme, but it would not appear old-fashioned.

1925–1937

By 1925 the Weimar Republic was no longer revolutionary; hopes for a new and better world had dimmed. The period of experimental architectural projects was drawing to a close and for the first time since the war buildings were actually under construction. Mies's most active period had already begun: his first post-war commission in 1924 was for a large house in Neubabelsberg, and in 1925 he built a group of low-cost apartments for the city of Berlin (page 36), in which, despite the exigencies of economy, plan, and fenestration, he achieved an effect of simple, unforced dignity.

During the years 1925–1929 he built three houses and a monument of brick, a material he had come to admire in Holland. He was the only modern architect to use brick at this time. His contemporaries, still under the influence of the machine esthetic, refused to do so because of its handcraft connotations, rough texture, and suggestion of mass rather than surface. Mies, with his Berlagian approach, appreciated the fact that brick was a structural material which need not be concealed. He liked the regular rhythm achieved by the repetition of a module and he enjoyed the craftsmanship involved in the coursing and bonding. His admiration led him to extraordinary measures: in order to insure the evenness of the bonding at corners and apertures, he calculated all dimensions in brick lengths and occasionally went so far as to separate the under-fired long bricks from the over-fired short ones, using the long in one dimension and the short in the other. Also characteristic are refinements such as the twisted purple clinker brick of the monument to Karl Liebknecht and Rosa Luxemburg (page 37) and the precise bonding of the imported Dutch brick in the Wolf house (pages 38–39). The latter, like the Lange house (pages 40–41), has a complex plan and an exterior of Schinkelesque serenity; while the monument bears some resemblance to a *Stijl* composition, although its overlapping rectangular forms do not interlock and they suggest weight rather than planes.

35

Municipal housing development, Afrikanischestrasse, Berlin. 1925

Monument to Karl Liebknecht and Rosa Luxemburg, Berlin. 1926. Destroyed

Wolf house, Guben, Germany. 1926

Wolf house. Terrace

Hermann Lange house, Krefeld, Germany. 1928. Badly damaged. View from garden

Hermann Lange house. Entrance

In 1926 Mies van der Rohe was appointed First Vice-President of the *Deutscher Werkbund*. His selection was no doubt largely due to the reputation he had gained through leadership of the *Novembergruppe* and the *Zehner Ring,* an architectural group formed to offset official prejudice against the modern movement. The *Werkbund* had been founded in 1907 by leading architects and industrialists. Its purpose was to improve the quality of German industrial design in order to compete more advantageously with the English, who were both more efficient and more progressive. By 1926 it had become the most powerful European influence for quality in modern design. The first of its expositions to have world-wide influence was held at Cologne in 1914, where Henry van de Velde built his famous theater and Walter Gropius, his machine hall.

The second exposition, a group of houses called the *Weissenhofsiedlung,* was held in 1927 at Stuttgart under the direction of Mies. He originally conceived it as a unified community (opposite), the buildings to be ranged on a terraced hill in uneven rows with pedestrian thoroughfares, instead of streets, opening into generous squares. But since the city of Stuttgart wished to sell the individual houses at the close of the exposition, the plan was executed as a group of free-standing buildings.

Mies invited the foremost European modern architects to participate. Three of them in particular had independently paralleled his period of radical experimentation: Gropius in Germany, Le Corbusier in France and Oud in Holland. Mies's selection of these men, now recognized as the architectural leaders of the twenties, shows his unusual ability as a critic. The *Weissenhofsiedlung* proved to be the most important group of buildings in the history of modern architecture. They demonstrated conclusively that the various architectural elements of the early post-war years had merged into a single stream. A new international order had been born. Except for the work of Frank Lloyd Wright, whose influence was felt by every architect represented at Stuttgart, all modern architecture of consequence in the Western world at that time was consonant with this order. It was no wonder that critics and architects alike wrote about the new "international architecture," or as Henry-Russell Hitchcock and I called it in 1932—on the insistence of Alfred Barr—the "Inter-

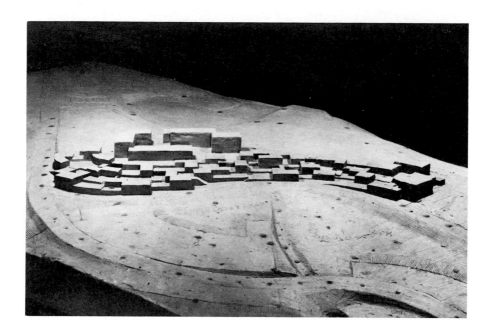

Project: *Weissenhofsiedlung,* Stuttgart, Germany. 1925. Model of early scheme

national Style." The work at Stuttgart shared so many disciplines and similarities that it deserved the appellation "style" as truly as the Gothic or the Romanesque.

This international order was based on a new appreciation of the technical and structural inventions of the previous century. Its esthetic characteristics are: 1) the regularity of skeleton structure as an ordering force in place of axial symmetry; 2) the treatment of exteriors as weightless, non-supporting skins rather than as heavy solids, obedient to gravity; 3) the use of color and structural detail in place of applied ornament.

The flexibility of skeleton construction was demonstrated by Mies in his apartment house (pages 46–47). By the use of movable partitions he created twelve apartments, all differently arranged, for each of the two basic units. Despite the complex interior, the exterior design is so quiet that one is apt, at first glance, to miss the subtle proportions of the window bands and the stairwell.

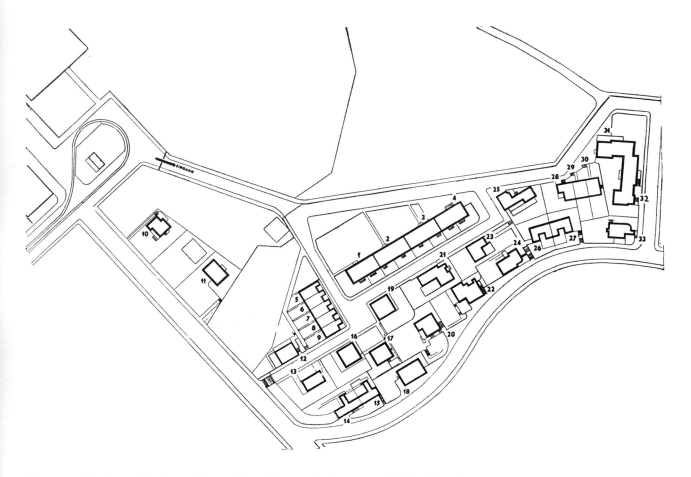

Weissenhofsiedlung, Werkbund Exposition, Stuttgart, Germany. 1927. Site plan

1-4	Mies van der Rohe	20	Hans Poelzig
5-9	J.J.P. Oud	21-22	Richard Döcker
10	Victor Bourgeois	23-24	Max Taut
11-12	Adolf G. Schneck	25	Adolf Rading
13-15	Le Corbusier with Pierre Jeanneret	26-27	Josef Frank
16-17	Walter Gropius	28-30	Mart Stam
18	Ludwig Hilberseimer	31-32	Peter Behrens
19	Bruno Taut	33	Hans Scharoun

Weissenhofsiedlung

Apartment house, *Weissenhofsiedlung*, Stuttgart, Germany. 1927. Street façade

Apartment house, *Weissenhofsiedlung,* Garden façade

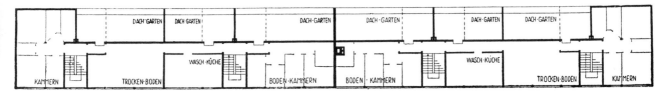

Fourth Floor

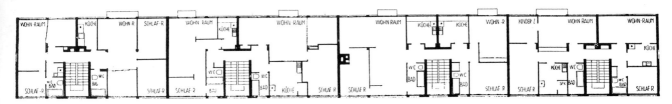

Third floor

Second floor

Ground floor

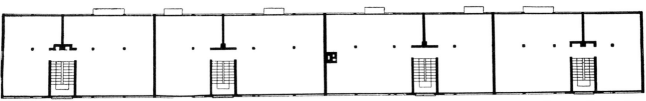

Construction system

Apartment house, *Weissenhofsiedlung*

Mies van der Rohe has also applied his architectural principles to exhibition installation and has given this field new importance, turning the display of objects into an art. For the *Werkbund* Exposition of 1927 he designed the first of several famous installations (page 51) with his brilliant partner, Lilly Reich, who soon became his equal in this field.

As in architecture, he has always been guided by his personal motto, "less is more." The sparseness of his installations focuses attention on each object and makes the arrangement of the objects all-important. Mies is a master at placing things in space. A minimum of stands, cases and partitions are disposed with studied exactness to achieve the maximum individual and total effect. Wherever possible the architectural schemes are based on the materials displayed: for example, the walls of the glass exhibit (page 51) are glass; those of the silk exhibit (page 50) are silk. He has designed each showcase and stand with the same simplicity and attention to detail that characterize his architecture.

Mies's concern with every object exhibited led him to design his first and most famous chair, known as the MR chair (page 56), which was exhibited in the *Exposition de la Môde* in 1927 (page 50). Its hard shiny chromium surface was used to set off the soft folds of silk curtains. This tubular cantilevered chair, with its elegant semicircular supports, was an immediate success and has been copied all over the world. In fact, until he left Germany, Mies derived a large part of his income from a patent on the cantilever principle.

The curving contours of Mies's chairs are always generous and calm. Being a large man, he thinks of furniture in ample terms. The Barcelona chair (page 54), the most beautiful piece of furniture he has ever designed, is large enough for two people to sit in. The single curve of the back crossing the reverse curve of the seat expresses "chair" better than any other contemporary model.

As always, Mies's impeccable craftsmanship plays an important part in his furniture design. Everything is calculated to the last millimeter: the width and thickness of the strap metal and the radius of the curves at the joints; the width and spacing of the leather strapping, the size of the upholstery buttons, the fineness of the welting and the proportions of the leather rectangles on the cushions.

Silk exhibit, *Exposition de la Môde,* **Berlin. 1927. In collaboration with Lilly Reich**

Materials and colors: black, orange and red
velvet; gold, silver, black and lemon-yellow
silk

Exhibit of the glass industry, Werkbund Exposition, Stuttgart, Germany. 1927

Materials and colors: chairs, white chamois
and black cowhide; table, rosewood; floor,
black and white linoleum; walls, etched, clear
and gray opaque glass

51

Silk exhibit, German section, International Exposition, Barcelona, Spain. 1929. In collaboration with Lilly Reich

Mining exhibit, *Deutsches Volk, Deutsche Arbeit* Exposition, Berlin. 1934

"Barcelona" chair. 1929

Couch, coffee table. 1930

MR chairs. 1926

"Tugendhat" chair. 1930

"Brno" chair. 1930

During the years 1928–29, Mies worked on four projects for office buildings, all of which reveal simplifications and refinements of his early experiments in glass buildings. His development is particularly visible in the competition entry for an office building on the triangular site opposite the Friedrichstrasse Station (page 62)—the same site for which, ten years before, he had designed his jagged prismatic plan (page 25). In another competition entry, a design for the remodeling of the Alexanderplatz in Berlin (page 64), he ignored the closed, almost classical plan proposed by the city, thus eliminating himself from consideration by the jury; but he created an open asymmetrical area of far more impressive proportions, achieving order not by a symmetrical or even rectangular arrangement, but by a discriminating grouping of buildings around a free-standing 17-story skyscraper.

The culminating achievement of Mies's European career was the German Pavilion for the International Exposition at Barcelona in 1929 (pages 66–74). The Barcelona Pavilion has been acclaimed by critics and architects alike as one of the milestones of modern architecture. It is truly one of the few manifestations of the contemporary spirit that justifies comparison with the great architecture of the past, and it is lamentable that it existed for only one season. Here for the first time Mies was able to build a structure unhampered by functional requirements or insufficient funds. In doing so he incorporated many characteristics of his previous work, such as insistence on expert craftsmanship and rich materials, respect for the regular steel skeleton and preoccupation with extending walls into space. Critics have seen in the hovering roof and open plan a reflection of Frank Lloyd Wright's prairie houses; in the disposition of the walls, the influence of de Stijl; or in the elevation of the structure on a podium, a touch of Schinkel. But the important fact is that all of these elements were fused in the crucible of Mies's imagination to produce an original work of art.

The design is simultaneously simple and complex: its ingredients are merely steel columns and independent rectangular planes of various materials placed vertically as walls or horizontally as roofs; but they are disposed in such a way that space is channeled rather than confined—it is never stopped, but is allowed to flow continuously. The only

Project: Adam building, Leipzigerstrasse, Berlin. 1928

decorative elements besides the richness of materials are two rectangular pools and a statue by Georg Kolbe, and these are inseparable components of the composition.

The independent walls and flowing space are developments of motifs which Mies first evolved in the brick country house of 1923 (page 32), and on which he has been composing variations ever since. Sometimes this effect is only part of a larger design, as in the well-known Tugendhat house in Brno, Czechoslovakia of 1930 (pages 76–86), where space can be said to flow only on the main living floor. Here the overall plan, devised to meet the needs of a growing family, is closed rather than open.

The fame of this house, Mies's best-known design after the Barcelona Pavilion, rests largely on the handling of space and the use of materials in the living-dining area, now a classic modern interior. A huge area measuring 50 by 80 feet, this main room is articulated by a straight wall of onyx and a curved wall of Macassar ebony which define the four functional areas: living room, dining room, library and entrance hall. The feeling of endless, flowing space is increased by the two outer walls, composed entirely of glass, which command a view of the sloping garden and the city beyond. At the press of a button alternating panes slide into the floor, further uniting interior and exterior. At night raw silk curtains cover the glass walls from floor to ceiling, enhancing the luxuriousness of the interior by their color and texture.

The elegance of this room derives not only from its size and the simple beauty of its design, but from the contrast of rich materials and the exquisite perfection of details. With a scrupulousness unparalleled in our day, Mies personally designed every visible element even to the lighting fixtures, the curtain track holders and the heating pipes.

Equally unusual is the unique manner in which he has incorporated the arrangement of furniture into the over-all design. The relation of one piece of furniture to another, of one group to another, and of the groups to the walls and partitions is so carefully calculated as to seem inevitable. No other important contemporary architect cares so much about placing furniture. Mies gives as much thought to placing chairs in a room as other architects do to placing buildings around a square.

Project: bank building, Stuttgart, Germany. 1928

Project: office building, Friedrichstrasse, Berlin. 1929. Second scheme

Project: remodeling of Alexanderplatz, Berlin. 1928

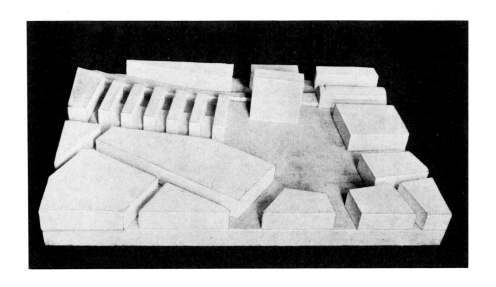

Project: remodeling of Alexanderplatz, Berlin

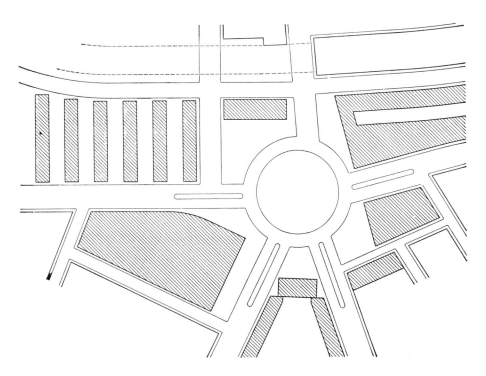

Project: remodeling of Alexanderplatz, Berlin

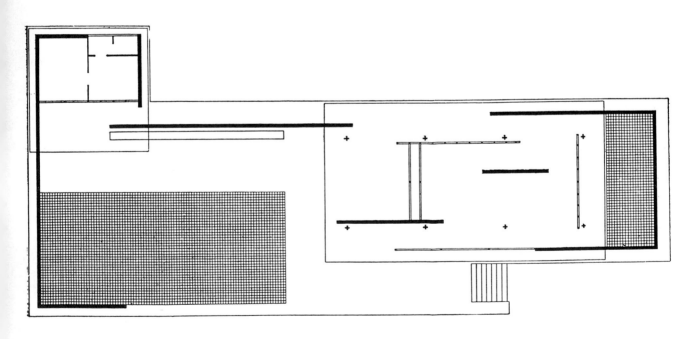

Barcelona Pavilion. Plan

German Pavilion, International Exposition, Barcelona, Spain. 1929. Demolished

Materials and colors:

Base and light-colored walls: Roman travertine. Walls around sculpture pool: green Tinian marble. Partition at rear of hall: gray transparent glass. Double panel with light source between: etched glass. Partition between sculpture pool and hall: bottle green transparent glass. Free-standing partition in hall: onyx. Pool lining: black glass

Barcelona Pavilion

Barcelona Pavilion

Barcelona Pavilion

Barcelona Pavilion

Barcelona Pavilion

Barcelona Pavilion

Barcelona Pavilion

German Electrical Industries exhibit, International Exposition, Barcelona, Spain. 1929. Demolished

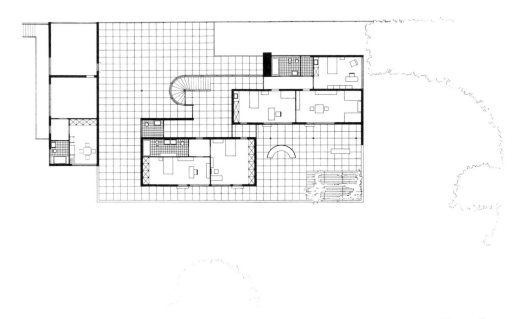

Upper floor

Tugendhat house. Plans

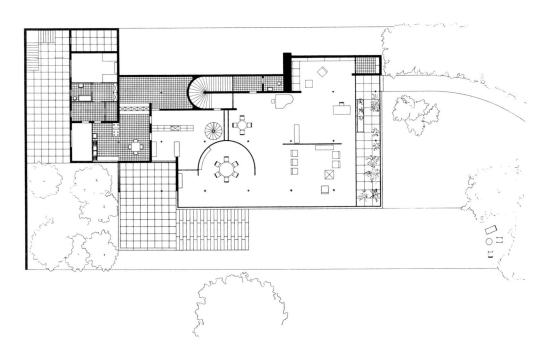

Lower floor

Tugendhat house, Brno, Czechoslovakia. 1930. Badly damaged. View from garden

Tugendhat house. View from street

Tugendhat house. Entrance

Tugendhat house. Study and living room

Materials and colors:
Living room wall: tawny gold and white cnyx.
Dining room wall: striped black and pale brown Macassar ebony. Curtains: black and beige raw silk, white velvet. Rug: natural wool. Floor: white linoleum. Chairs: white vellum, natural pigskin and pale green cowhide upholstery

80

Tugendhat house. Living room

Tugendhat house. Living room

Tugendhat house. Dining room

Tugendhat house. Living room

Tugendhat house. Living room

Tugendhat house. Foyer

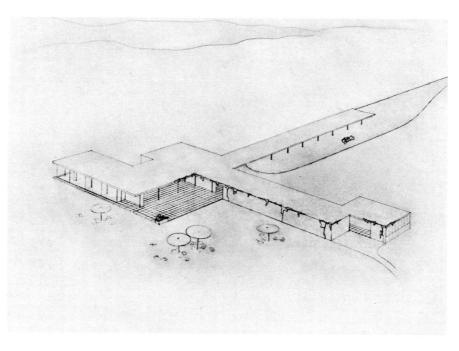

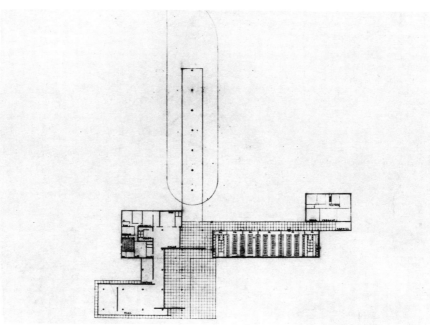

Project: Country Club, Krefeld, Germany. 1930

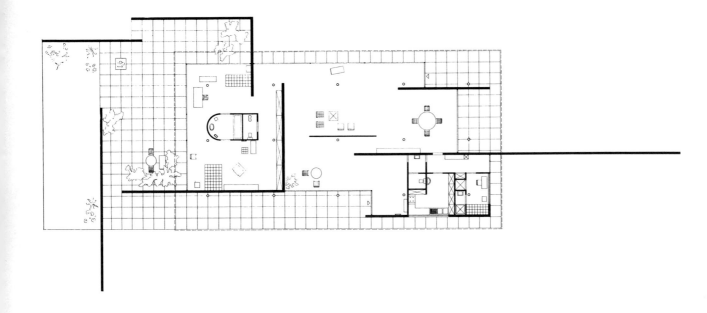

House, Berlin Building Exposition. Plan

House, Berlin Building Exposition, Berlin. 1931. Demolished

House, Berlin Building Exposition. Living Room

House, Berlin Building Exposition. Dining room

House, Berlin Building Exposition. Enclosed garden

House, Berlin Building Exposition. Bedroom

93

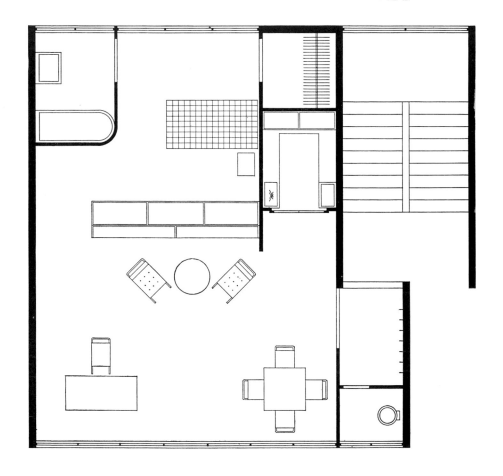

Apartment for a bachelor. Plan

Apartment for a bachelor, Berlin Building Exposition, Berlin. 1931. Demolished. Living and dining room

From 1931 to 1938 Mies developed a series of projects for "court-houses" (pages 97–105) in which the flow of space is confined within a single rectangle formed by the outside walls of court and house conjoined. The houses themselves are shaped variously as L's, T's or I's and their exterior walls, except those forming part of the outside rectangle, are all of glass. All of the projects are rectangular except one (page 104), a virtuoso study in which Mies introduced a daring diagonal axis inside rectangular frame and successfully avoided oblique and acute angles by curving the partitions.

During the same years Mies designed five adaptations of the court-house idea for clients (pages 110–121), but only one of them—a small L house on a narrow Berlin lot (page 110)—was ever built. In 1934, on a vacation in the Tyrol, he sketched a romantic court-house for himself at the entrance to a mountain pass (page 107). The plan, impossible to comprehend from the drawing, is ordered within a V-shaped wall, the legs of which extend into the slope of the mountains on either side of the pass. In the angle of the V lies the court, rectangular in shape and bounded on two sides by the glass walls of an L-shaped house. The two ends of the house L are also of glass, and since they are at the same time part of the main walls, they constitute the only apertures in them. This use of a single large opening, asymmetrically placed, in each main wall of a structure is a solution Mies favors for elevations of a one-story masonry building; and he has studied the proportioning of the opening in several deceptively casual sketches (page 108).

In 1933 Mies was invited with twenty-nine other architects to enter the competition for the new Reichsbank in Berlin. His design was the only modern one among the six prize winners (pages 122–127). It was also the most ordered and monumental, containing as it did an enormous main lobby, 350 feet long by 50 feet wide and 30 feet high, with a grand staircase worthy of a Baroque palace. The plan, oddly enough, was symmetrical, while those of its Neo-Classical and Neo-Baroque competitors, which one would have expected to be so, were influenced by the irregular shape of the city lot. Four years later he designed another project with a similar splayed symmetrical plan, an administration building for the silk industry in Krefeld (pages 128–130).

Sketch for a court-house. c. 1931

Mies's European career reached its zenith in the early thirties. In 1930 he was appointed Director of the Bauhaus School in Dessau at the instigation of the former Director, Walter Gropius; in 1931 he was accorded the signal honor of being named a member of the Prussian Academy of Arts and Sciences. But the following year, because of the local Nazi regime, he was forced to move the Bauhaus from Dessau. It was re-established in Berlin where it existed precariously until he decided to close it in the fall of 1933. With the Nazis hostile to everything he represented, Mies began to look toward the more hospitable climate of America. He left Germany in the summer of 1937, and in 1944 he became an American citizen.

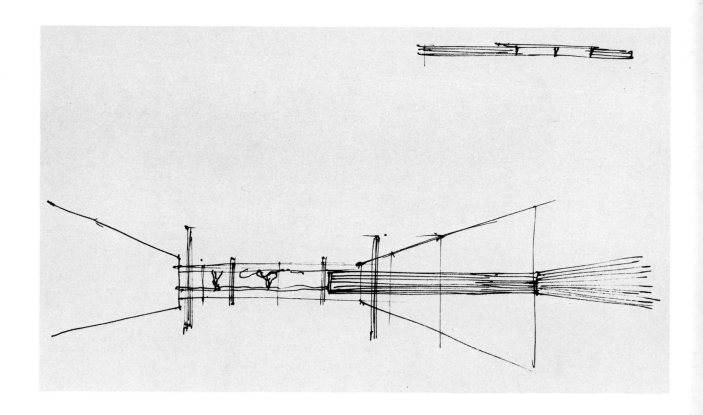

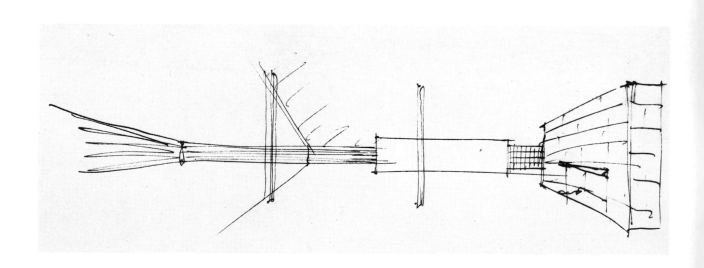

Sketches for court-houses. c. 1931

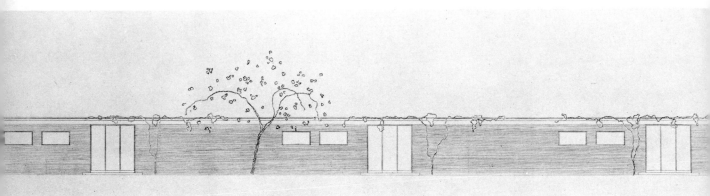

Project: row houses. 1931

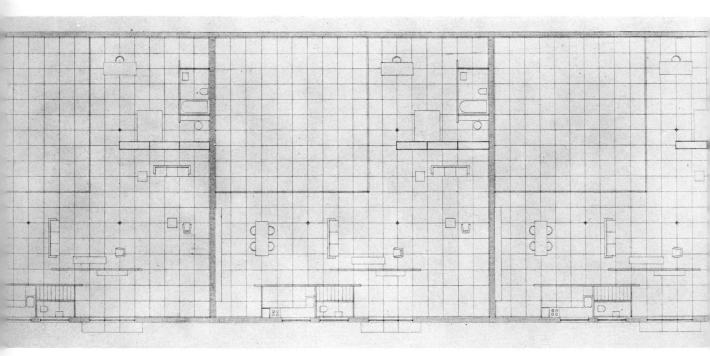

Plan for row houses

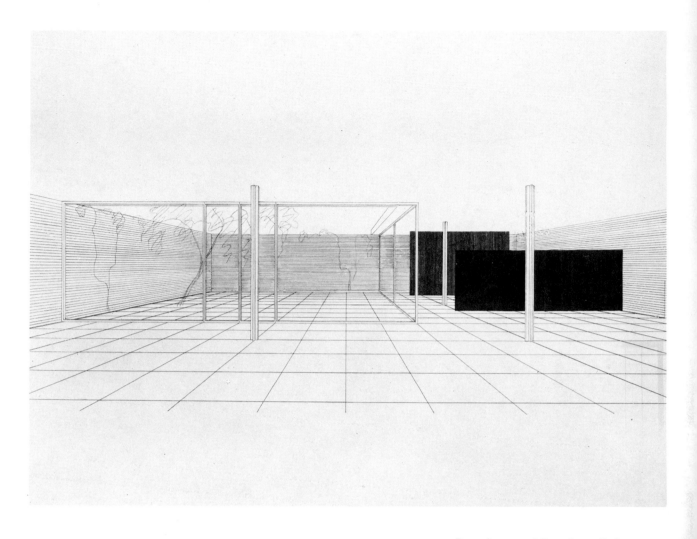

Row houses. View from living room

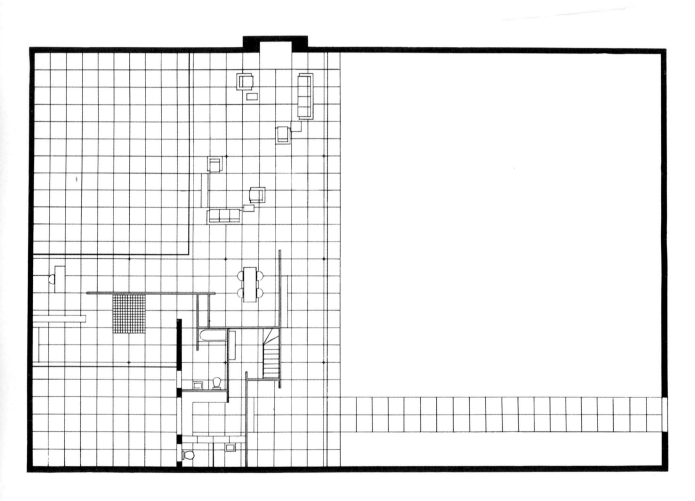

Project: house with three courts. 1934

102

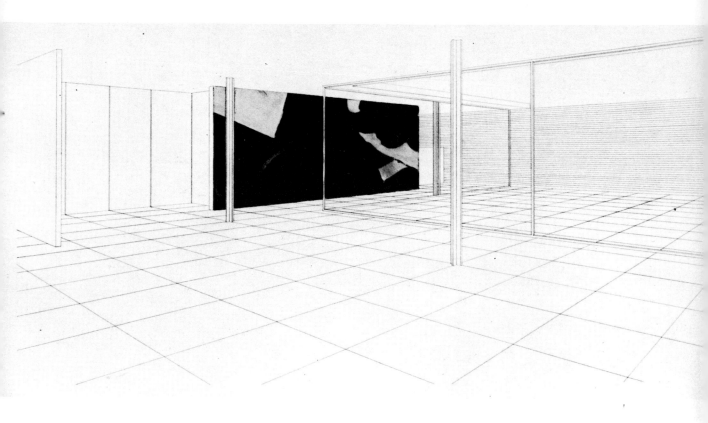

House with three courts. Perspective of bedroom wing

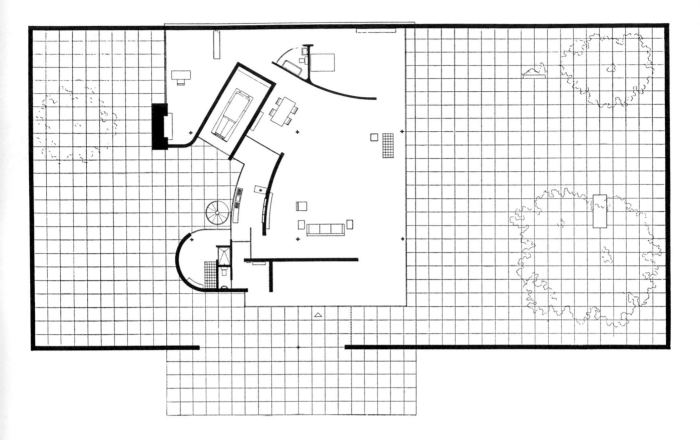

Project: court-house with garage. 1934

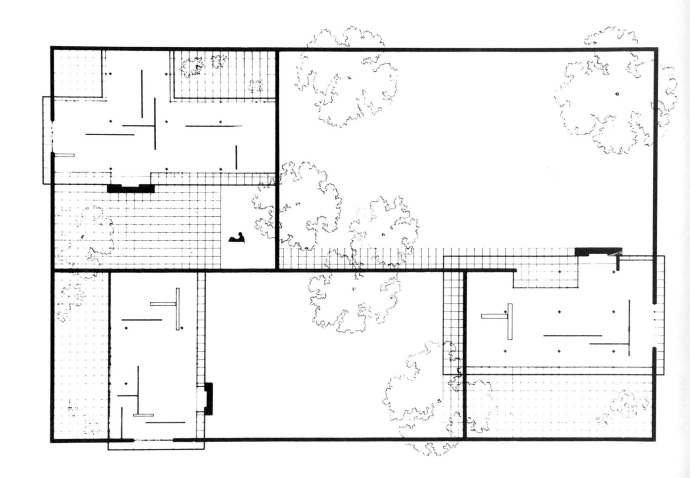

Project: group of court-houses. 1938

Mountain house. Elevation

Project: mountain house for the architect, Tyrol, Austria. 1934

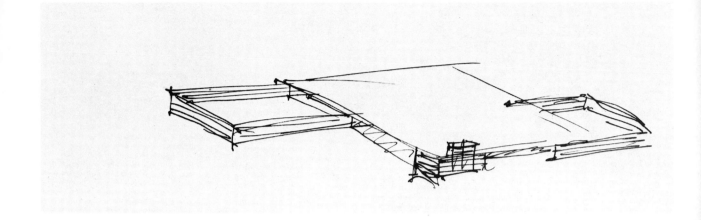

Sketch for a court-house. c. 1934

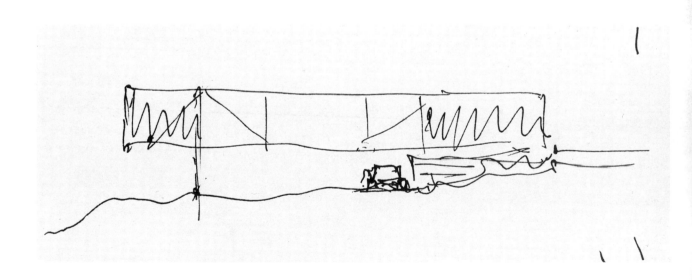

Sketch for a glass house on a hillside. c. 1934

opposite: Sketches for country houses. c. 1934

Lemcke house, Berlin. 1932. Terrace

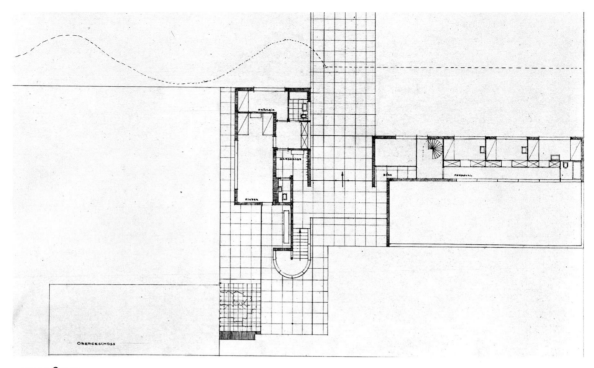

upper floor

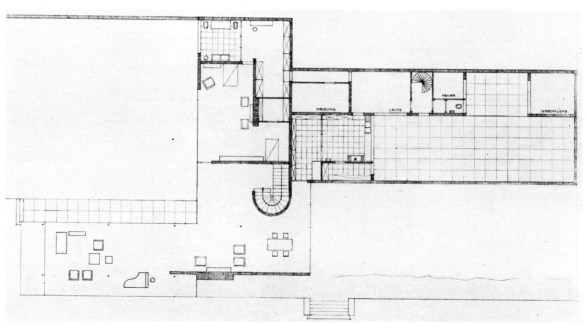

lower floor

Project: Gericke house, Wannsee, Berlin. 1930

111

Gericke house. Perspective from sunken garden

Gericke house. Perspective from dining room

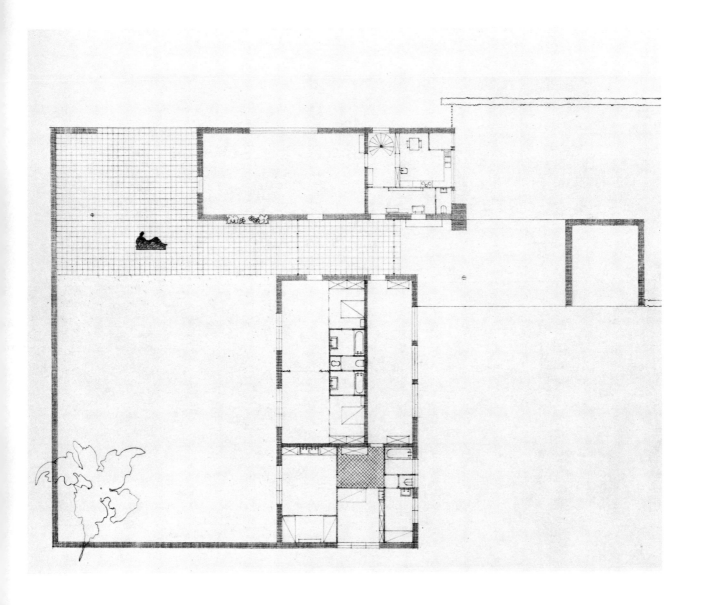

Project: first Ulrich Lange house, Krefeld, Germany. 1935

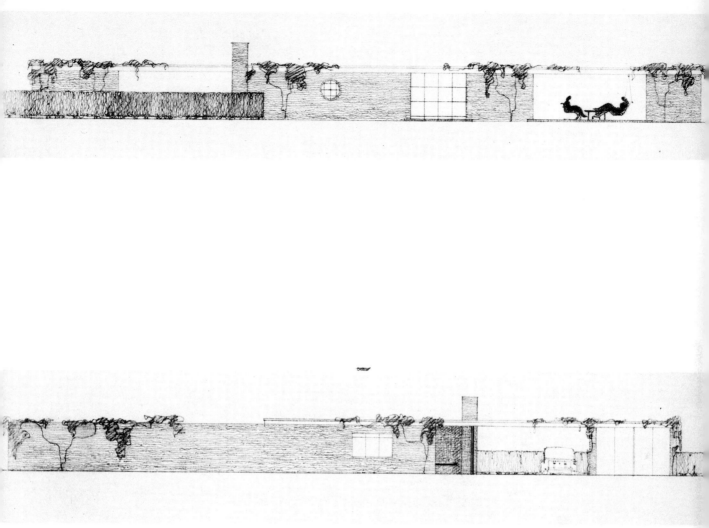

First Ulrich Lange house. Elevations

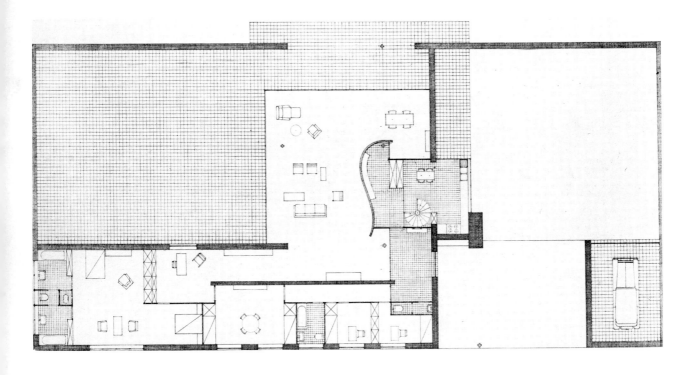

Project: second Ulrich Lange house, Krefeld, Germany. 1935

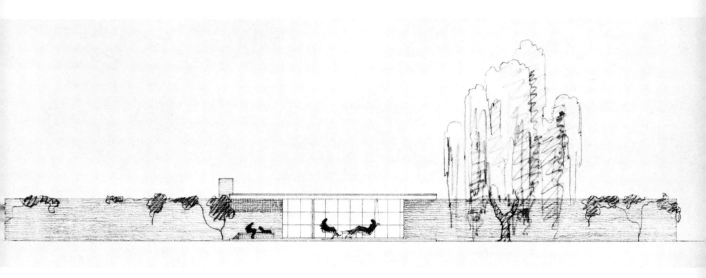

Second Ulrich Lange house. Elevations

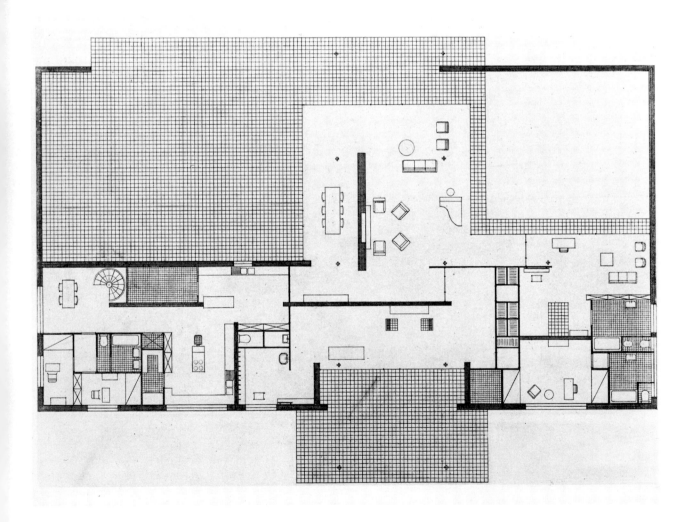

Project: Hubbe house, Magdeburg, Germany. 1935

118

Hubbe house. Living room

Hubbe house. Terrace

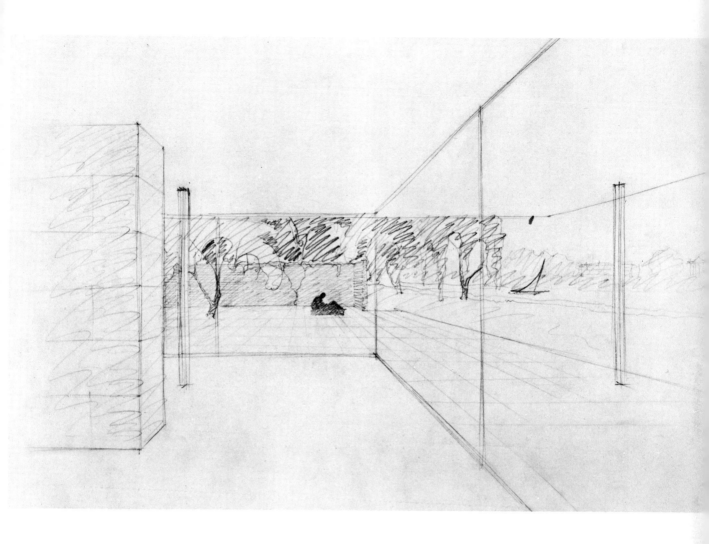

Hubbe house. Terrace

Project: Reichsbank, Berlin. 1933. Model

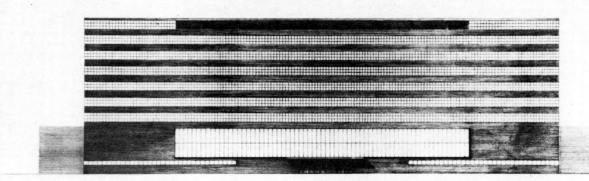

Reichsbank. Elevation

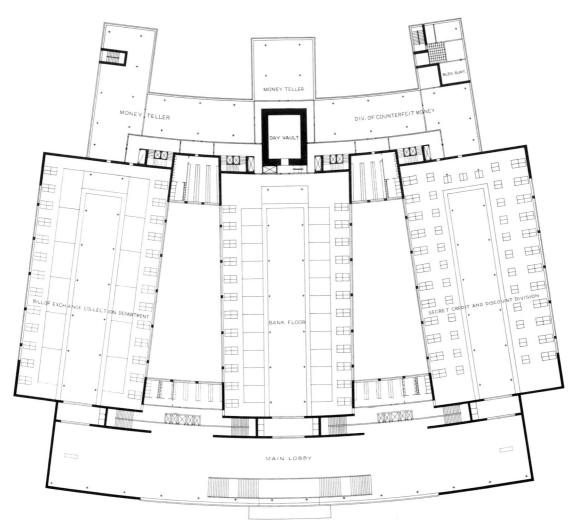

Reichsbank. First floor

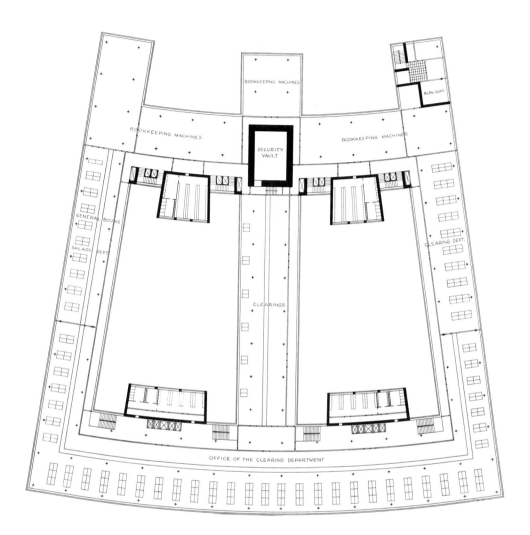

Reichsbank. Typical floor

Reichsbank

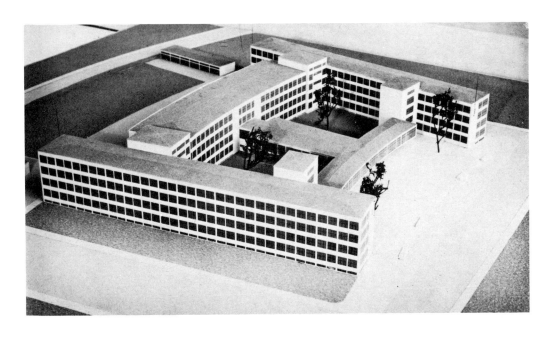

Project: administration building for the silk industry, Krefeld, Germany. 1937. Model

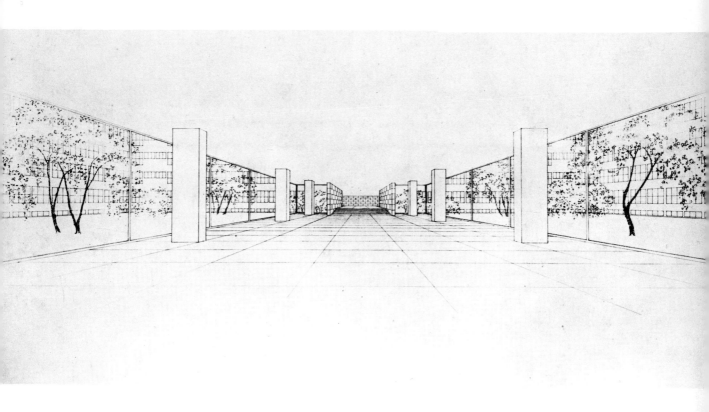

Administration building for the silk industry. Main hall

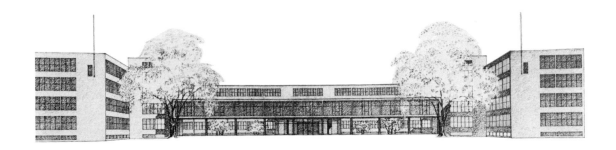

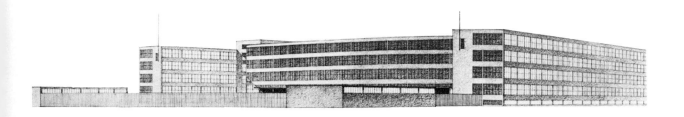

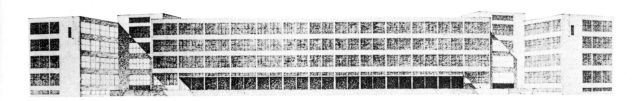

Administration building for the silk industry. Perspectives

1937–1947

One of Mies van der Rohe's main creative works in America, and one of the most important of his entire career, is the new campus for Illinois Institute of Technology. He became Director of Architecture of Armour Institute, as it was then called, in 1938 at the suggestion of the Chicago architect, John A. Holabird. Soon afterward President Henry T. Heald, Mies's staunch supporter, awarded him the commission for the campus. No other modern architect has had an opportunity to design on so large a scale. When completed it will be one of the rare executed examples of group planning by a great contemporary artist. (See page 134 for final scheme.)

In the first scheme (pages 132–133), begun in 1939, Mies planned to remove the long center street from the rectangular site—eight blocks in Chicago's South Side—in order to dispose a unified group of large buildings around an open plaza. To increase the sense of space without destroying the frame of the plaza, many of the peripheral buildings were to have been raised on exposed steel columns; and the two fan-shaped auditoriums were to act as diverting accents in the rectangular plan.

However, since it was not considered feasible to remove the main thoroughfare, this scheme was discarded in favor of the present one (page 134), which incorporates clusters of smaller buildings within the previous symmetrical plan. Ironically, it was later decided that the street could be removed, but only after construction had begun.

Mies's basic concept can be seen most clearly in the series of schemes he worked out for an ideal site devoid of crisscross streets (pages 136–137). Each plan is immediately comprehensible: the buildings are always grouped around a central plaza in such a way that they create a continuous interchange of open and closed spaces. This interwoven effect is achieved by the simple but highly original device of sliding adjacent units past one another, rather than placing them side by side. The plazas thus defined, without being closed, combine the intimacy of the courts,

perspective

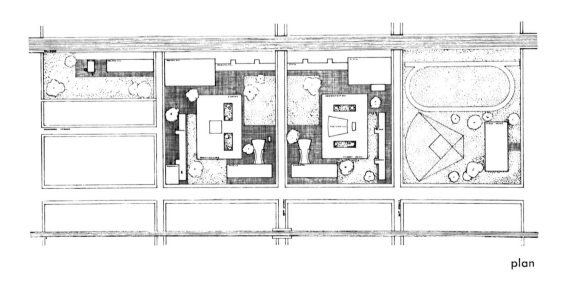

plan

Project: Illinois Institute of Technology, Chicago. 1939. Preliminary scheme

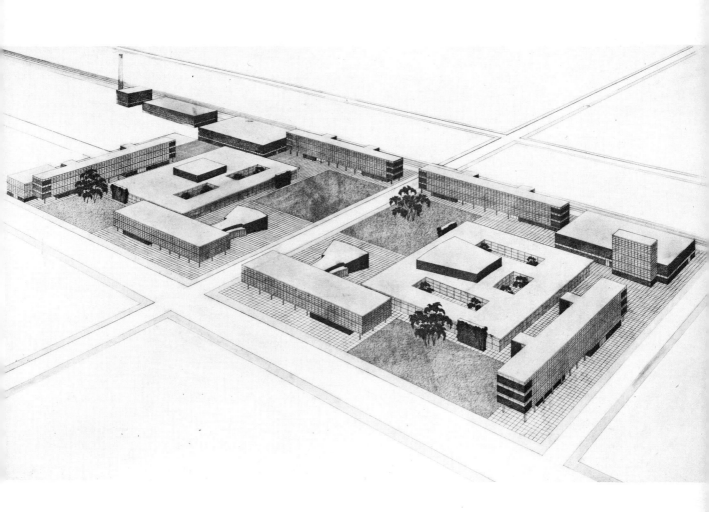

Project: Illinois Institute of Technology, Chicago. 1939. Preliminary scheme

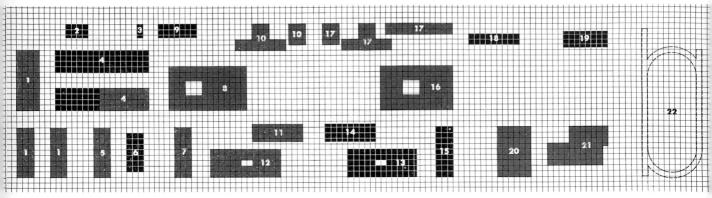

Project: Illinois Institute of Technology, Chicago. 1940. Final scheme

Gray denotes future buildings; black denotes completed buildings or completed portions of buildings in 1953.

1. Armour Research Foundation Research Laboratory
2. Boiler Plant
3. Central Vault
4. A.R.F. Engineering Research
5. Institute of Gas Technology Laboratory
6. Institute of Gas Technology
7. Architecture and Design
8. Student Union and Auditorium
9. Minerals and Metals Research
10. Electrical Engineering and Physics
11. Lewis Institute
12. Mechanical Engineering

13. Chemical Engineering and Metallurgy
14. Chemistry
15. Alumni Memorial Hall
16. Library and Administration
17. Civil Engineering and Mechanics
18. Association of American Railroads Building
19. Association of American Railroads Laboratory
20. Field House
21. Gymnasium and Swimming Pool
22. Athletic Field

Illinois Institute of Technology, Chicago. 1940. Final Scheme

Left, Alumni Memorial Hall; center, Chemical Engineering and Metallurgy Building; right, Chemistry Building. Associated in design of Chemistry Building were Friedman, Alschuler & Sincere; in others Holabird and Root

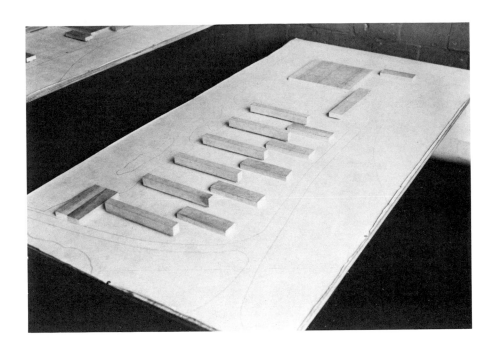

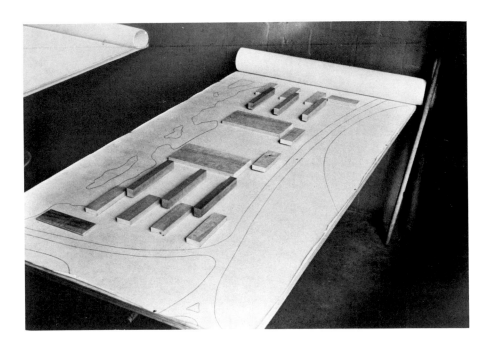

Projects: three arrangements of I.I.T. buildings on an imaginary park site

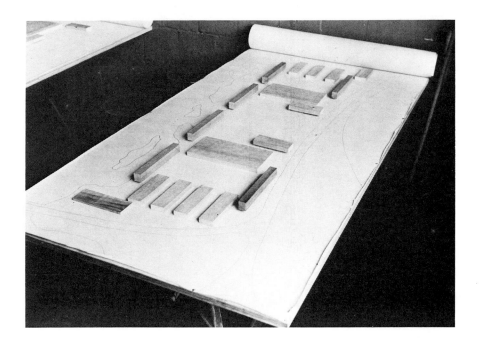

say, at Oxford, with the clarity of a classically arranged campus such as Jefferson's University of Virginia. Unlike the Jefferson campus, order is not dependent on axial grouping, but on a subtler symmetry deriving from the fact that every building, no matter what its size, is based on the same cubic bay, 24 feet by 24 feet by 12 feet high, and that the spaces between the buildings are regulated by the same 24-foot module. This basic rhythm is further stressed on the exterior walls by the brick or glass panels, 24 feet by 12 feet, each framed by the exposed steel structure. Such regularity could easily become monotonous, were it not that the buildings are varied in length, width and height as well as in the patterning of the exterior panels.

The unified bay system also prevails in the final design, although the rhythm is broadened in the most important unit, the Library and Administration building (pages 139 -146). Here the length of each bay is extended to 64 feet and the height to 30 feet. This building, possibly Mies's greatest single design, has a rectangular plan of the utmost simplicity.

What is difficult to grasp from the drawings is its size: 300 feet by 200 feet by 30 feet high. The bays are almost three times the size of the usual ones and the panes of glass on the entrance façade, 18 feet by 12 feet, are the largest that have ever been used. In the administration section, which occupies a little over half of the entire space, including the court, the offices are separated by 8-foot high partitions, so that nothing interrupts the enormous space between these and the 30-foot roof except a floating mezzanine cantilevered from four central columns. When constructed, this section will undoubtedly constitute one of the most impressive enclosed spaces in the history of modern architecture.

According to Mies, he would not have designed this building as he has without the example of Berlage. In it he has carried Berlage's theory of structural honesty to a logical extreme. Structural elements are revealed as are those of a Gothic cathedral: the inside and outside of the enclosing walls are identical in appearance, since the same steel columns and brick panels of the exterior are visible on the interior (pages 144–145). In other words, he has conceived the design in terms of steel channels and angles, I-beams and H-columns, just as a medieval design is conceived in terms of stone vaults and buttresses. But there is one major difference. He allows no decoration except that formed by the character and juxtaposition of the structural elements. And whereas the medieval architect relied on the collaboration of the sculptor and painter for his ultimate effect, Mies, so to speak, has had to perform the functions of all three professions. He joins steel to steel, or steel to glass or brick, with all the taste and skill that formerly went into the chiseling of a stone capital or the painting of a fresco.

The extraordinary subtleties of his detailing are most easily seen in photographs of two of the completed structures: the Minerals and Metals Research building (pages 147–148) and the Alumni Memorial building (pages 149–152). Inside the first, for example, the exposed beams and girders of the roof are arranged as carefully as those of a Renaissance beamed ceiling. In the Memorial building the amount of exposed structure is reduced by fireproofing. For this reason steel columns which would otherwise be visible are necessarily covered with concrete. The columns, in turn, are faced with mullions, but these are not permitted to masquer-

Project: Library and Administration Building, I.I.T. Chicago. 1944. Corner

ade as supports; instead they are stopped short just above the ground to reveal their true nature (page 151). This is a remarkable subtlety, as is the fact that the mullions, in framing the brick and glass panels, never merge with them, but are clearly separated by shadow-casting indentations, giving to the walls somewhat the quality of a relief (page 151). These indentations serve at the same time to minimize the inevitable unevenness of the brick panel edges by removing them from the straight mullions.

The same device is used in the hallway to separate the acoustical ceiling tiles from the walls, thus avoiding the crooked joint that might occur if the two planes met. Other notable refinements here are the rabbeted wooden glass frames and the expertly placed door handles and locks. The cantilevered stairway (page 152) is of such easy, weightless beauty that it is difficult to imagine the amount of thought behind it. Artistry, a vast accumulation of technical knowledge, and many hours of patient experimentation went into the exquisite details: the length and position of the wall railing, the simple joining of the outside railing to the stringer, and the clean articulated sweep of the unsupported flight of steps.

The simplicity of this particular architectural feature is characteristic of every campus building and symptomatic of the philosophy that shaped them. Mies expresses it in the German phrase *beinahe nichts*, "almost nothing." He does not want these buildings to be self-consciously architectural; he desires rather "the absence of architecture" and in its place he practices *Baukunst*, "the art of building." The structures executed so far may strike the untrained eye as unnecessarily barren since they are units of a larger design, the subtle beauty of which will emerge only when the whole is completed.

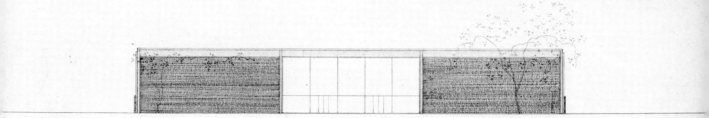

South elevation

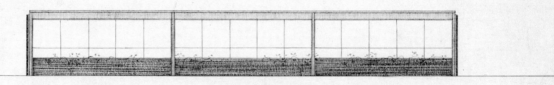

North elevation

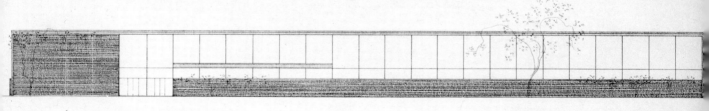

West elevation

Library and Administration Building

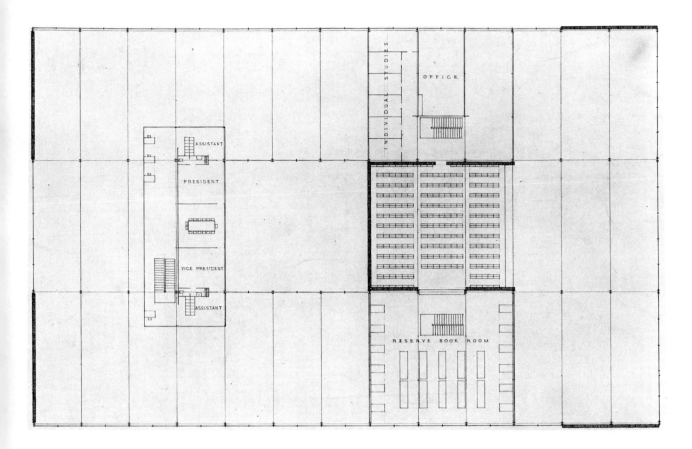

Library and Administration Building. Mezzanine

142

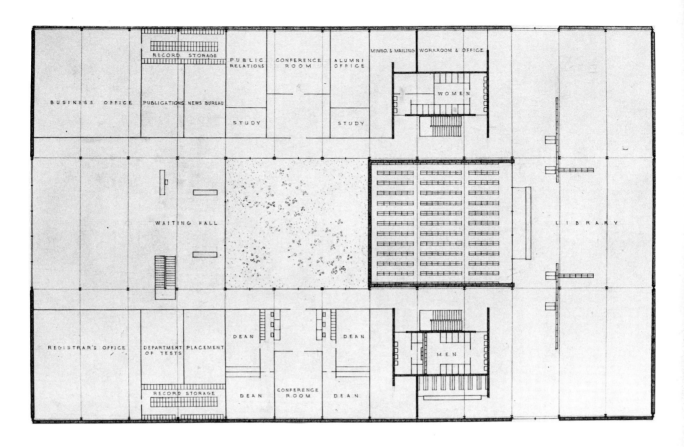

Library and Administration Building. Main floor

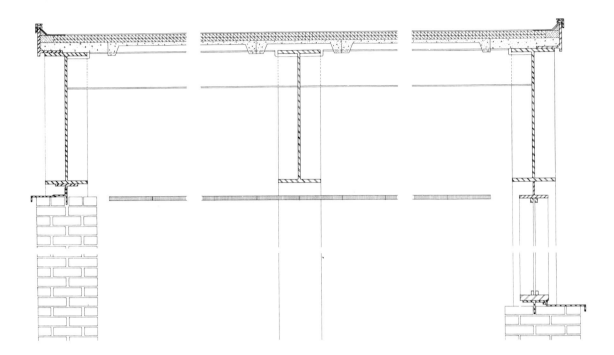

Typical vertical sections through roof and north and south walls

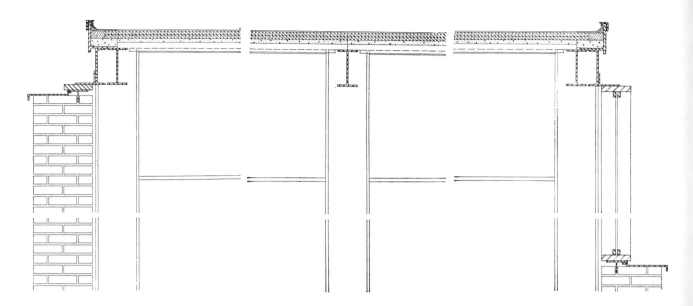

Typical vertical sections through roof and east and west walls

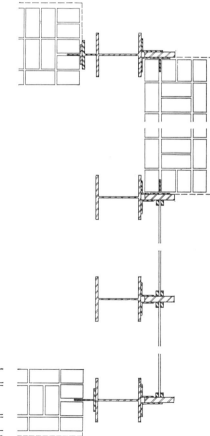

Typical horizontal sections through walls from northeast
corner to main south entrance

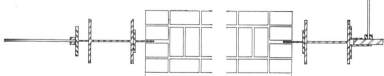

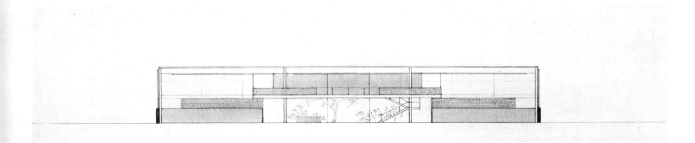

Section through administration offices

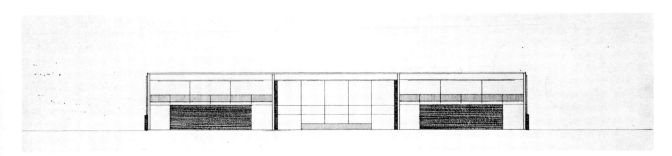

Section through library

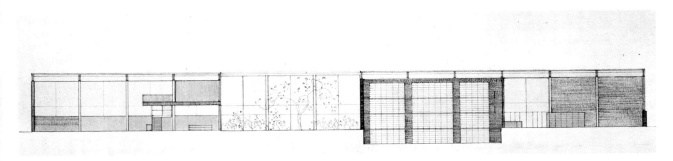

Longitudinal section

Library and Administration Building

Minerals and Metals Research Building, I.I.T., Chicago. Holabird and Root, Associated. 1942-43

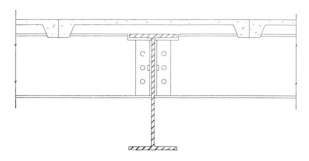

Vertical section through main girder

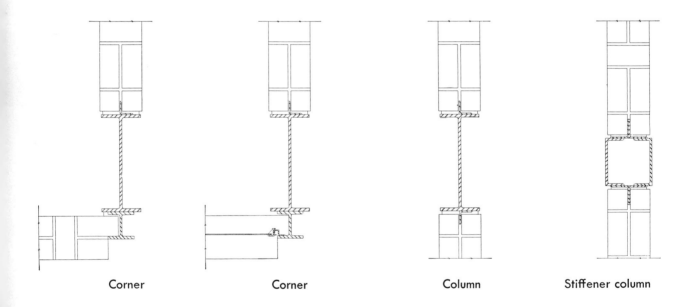

Corner   Corner   Column   Stiffener column

Minerals and Metals Research Building. Sections

Alumni Memorial Hall, I.I.T., Chicago. 1945-1946. Holabird and Root, Associated

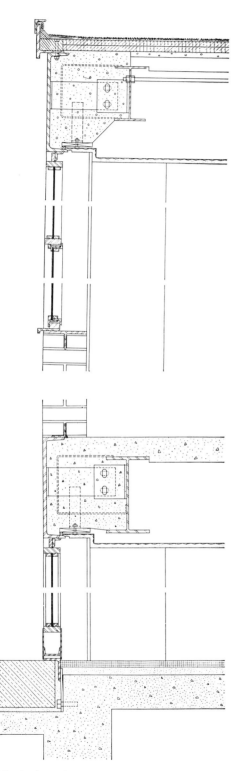

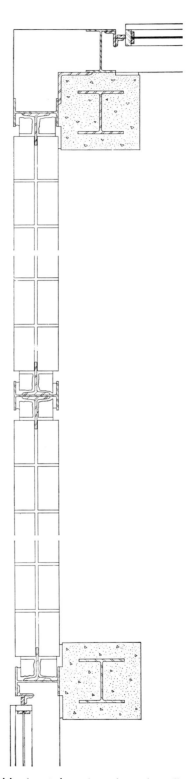

Vertical sections at entrance

Typical horizontal sections through wall

150

Alumni Memorial Hall. Details

151

Alumni Memorial Hall. Staircase

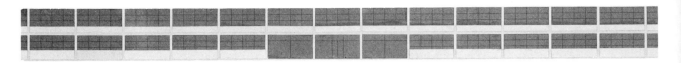

Concrete structure

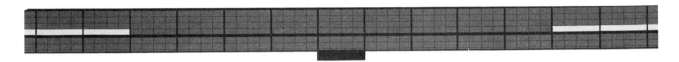

Steel structure

Steel structure

Steel structure

Chemical Engineering and Metallurgy Building, I.I.T., Chicago. 1941. Elevation studies

Mies van der Rohe came to America at the invitation of Mr. and Mrs. Stanley B. Resor, and during his first year here he projected a house for them in Wyoming (opposite). Like the Farnsworth house (pages 170–171), designed nine years later, it is conceived as a floating self-contained cage—a radical departure from his last European domestic projects, the earth-hugging court-houses. The Resor house, stretching across a river and resting on two stone bases, is sheathed in cypress planking, interrupted on each long side by an indented stretch of glass. The Farnsworth house with its continuous glass walls is an even simpler interpretation of the idea. Here the purity of the cage is undisturbed. Neither the steel columns from which it is suspended nor the independent floating terrace break the taut skin.

While carrying out his commissioned work, Mies has also found time to work on several projects that interest him. One of these is the use of plastics for furniture. He has sketched a group of moulded chairs which are called "conchoidal" because of their shell-like logarithmic curves (pages 158–159). These curves, arranged to fit the contours of the human body, also exploit the specific qualities of their material. Mies has utilized the freedom allowed by a mouldable substance to invent a series of entertaining and original shapes.

Another project, and one to which he has devoted a great deal of attention, is the museum for a small city (pages 160–164). This grew out of a desire to provide a setting for Picasso's great painting *Guernica*. It is the most elaborate expression of his theories governing the use of painting and sculpture with architecture. Just as in the Barcelona Pavilion and the house for the Berlin Building Exposition, works of art are used as an integral part of the design, but they are never required to sacrifice their independence. They enhance the architecture while the architecture enhances them.

In order that the arrangement of the museum may be as flexible as possible, the structure is reduced to its simplest terms: floor slab, columns, roof plate, free-standing partitions and exterior walls which, being of glass, scarcely function visibly as walls. The relative "absence of architecture" intensifies the individuality of each work of art and at the same time incorporates it into the entire design. Thus *Guernica* (page

Project: Resor house, Jackson Hole, Wyoming. 1938. View from interior

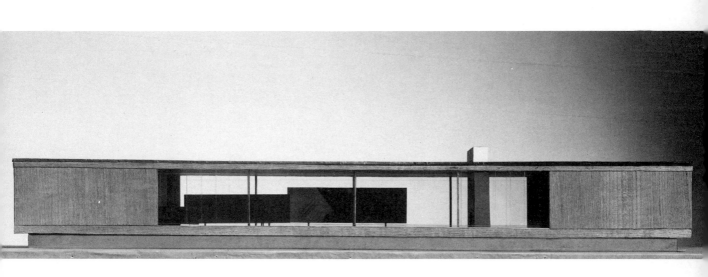

Resor house: model (not on original site)

155

164) is clearly an independent painting, while functioning architecturally as a screen that defines the space around it.

One of the museum's original features is the auditorium composed of free-standing partitions and an acoustical dropped ceiling (page 162). From this Mies has developed his most astounding new creation, the project for a concert hall (page 165), not yet completed, in which walls and ceilings are pulled apart and disposed within a trussed steel and

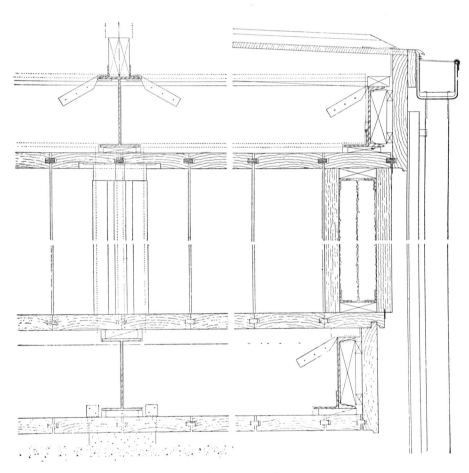

Vertical sections through column and outside wall

Resor house

glass cage. The concept of flowing horizontal space, first expressed in the brick country house of 1923 (page 32) and carried on to its triumphant culmination in the Barcelona Pavilion (page 67), now expands: space eddies in all directions among interior planes of subaqueous weightlessness.

These last projects, like all of his American work, are exerting an even greater influence today than did the famous five projects of the early twenties. It should be understood, however, that there is a qualitative difference between the influence of the two periods. In the twenties, the influence was that of a young pioneer, and its scope was restricted to the relatively few participants in the nascent movement. Now it is that of an established and polished master, still pioneering to be sure, but within the broader scope of a generally accepted tradition. Today as yesterday, his projects attract students and fellow architects by their daring, clarity, refinement and technical soundness; and his executed buildings are, in addition, striking examples of the finest possible craftsmanship. The impact of the sum of these qualities can already be detected in the work of other architects in Illinois, Massachusetts, Oregon and California.

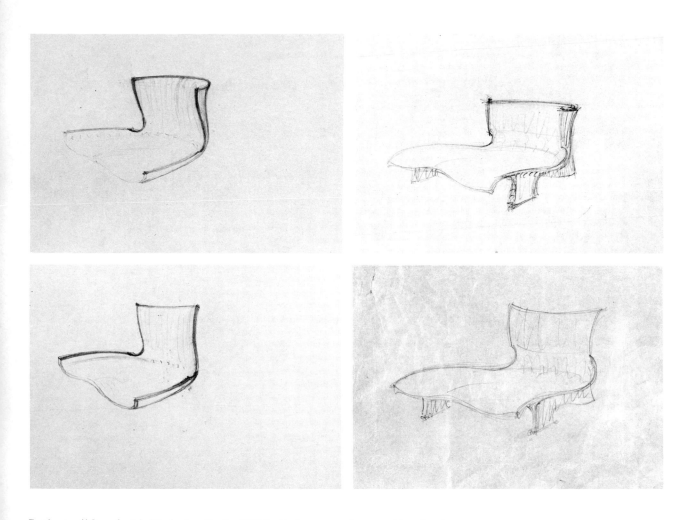

Projects: "Conchoidal" chairs. Early 1940s. To be manufactured in plastics

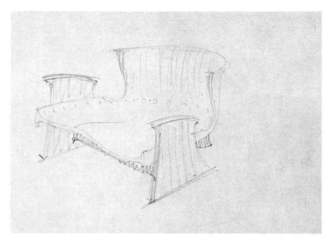

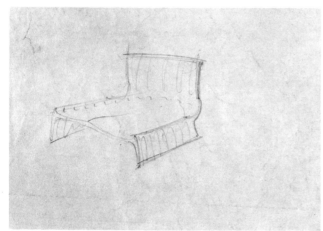

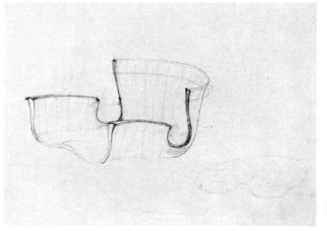

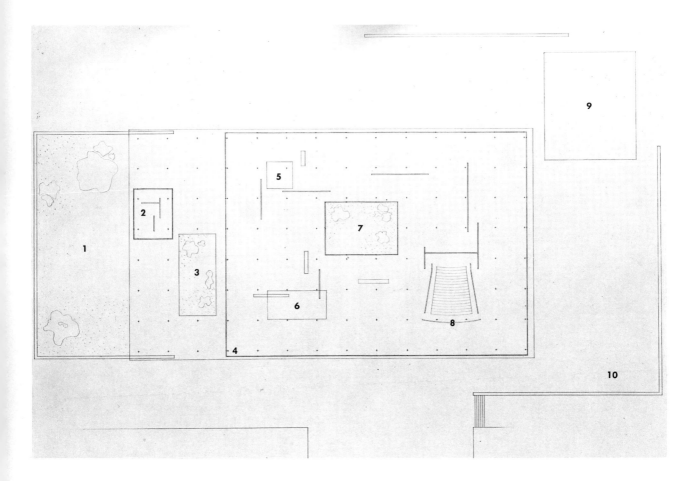

Project: Museum for a small city. 1942

"Two openings in the roof plate (3 & 7) admit light into an inner court (7) and into an open passage (3) through one end of the building. Outer walls (4) and those of the inner court are of glass. On the exterior, free-standing walls of stone would define outer courts (1) and terraces (10). Offices (2) and wardrobes would be free-standing. A shallow recessed area (5) is provided, around the edge of which small groups could sit for informal discussions. The auditorium (8) is defined by free-standing walls providing facilities for lectures, concerts and intimate formal discussions. The form of these walls and the shell hung above the stage would be dictated by the acoustics. The floor of the auditorium is recessed in steps of seat height, using each step as a continuous bench. Number (6) is the print department. Above it is a space for special exhibits. Number (9) is a pool." (bibl. 65)

To Lam Maron from Mies van der Rohe
Aug 27 1945.

Museum for a small city

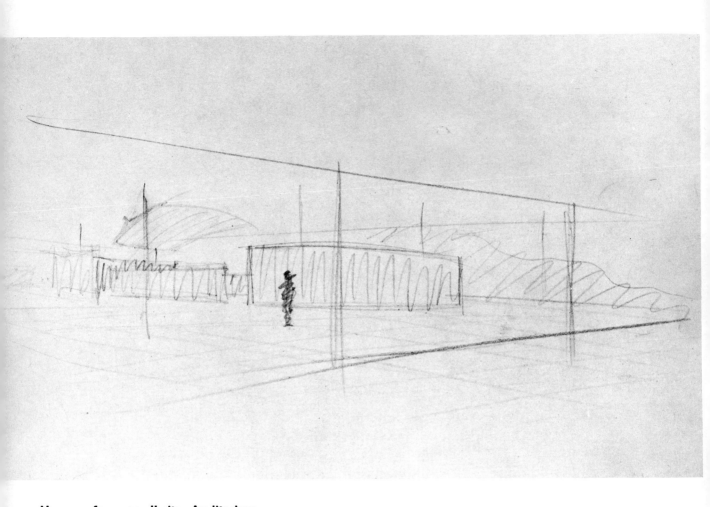

Museum for a small city. Auditorium

Museum for a small city. Interior perspective

Museum for a small city. Idea for an exhibition of Picasso's *Guernica*

Project: Concert Hall. 1942

Boiler Plant, I.I.T., Chicago. 1950. Sargent and Lundy, Frank J. Kornaker, Consultants

1948-1953

The six years since 1947 have been Mies's most productive years in actual building. Among the work completed during this period are the apartment houses at 860 Lake Shore Drive; the first all glass house in the world, for Dr. Edith Farnsworth; as well as a Chapel and a Boiler Plant for the Illinois Institute of Technology. In the first two of these buildings, as in some of his most recent projects, Mies has created new architectural expressions of great inventiveness based on technology.

The apartment houses at 860 Lake Shore Drive (pages 172–175) present a prototype for multi-story buildings which may become as influential in our era as Sullivan's skyscraper designs were in his. It is indeed Mies's first masterpiece in America. The two buildings, each 26 stories high, stand on a travertine platform, raised two stories off the ground on exposed columns. They are identical rectangles so disposed at right angles to one another that their joint silhouette is never the same. Seen from one angle, they are at once partially overlapping entities and, from another, separate web-like forms with open space between them. Every exterior wall of these two buildings is of glass, but in his use of projecting vertical steel I-beams welded to the façade Mies has replaced the flat surfaces of his earlier work with a subtle plasticity.

Structurally these projecting elements serve as wind braces and as mullions; visually they create a surface relief of solids and voids not found in the taut skin of his early buildings. The continuation of the mullions to the roofline extends the rhythm which the mullions create and makes a final ornamental note against the skyline.

The house for Dr. Edith Farnsworth (pages 170–171) is a study in the relationship between supporting and supported elements. Eight steel columns are welded to the fascias of the floor and roof planes. These fascias touch and by-pass the columns but do not rest *on* them, so that the house appears to be slung between the vertical supports. This structural purity is contrasted with the sumptuous materials used throughout

Promontory Apartments, Chicago. 1949. Pace Associates, and Holsman, Holsman, Klekamp and Taylor, Associated

the house: floors of Italian travertine, raw silk curtains and primavera wood cabinets.

The execution of proposed buildings for I.I.T. has progressed. In the Chapel (page 176) and the Boiler Plant (page 166), Mies's concern for the refinement of technological character continues. Although these are not buildings for educational purposes, and in spite of the differences of size and function, they are related to the I.I.T. campus by similarity of proportion and structural detail. The façades of the Boiler Plant are steel frames filled with buff colored brick panels which incorporate a variety of mechanical units. In subjecting these mechanical elements to an architectural discipline, wholly absent from conventional solutions to such utilitarian problems, Mies has made architecture of a boiler plant.

The projected Architecture and Design Building (pages 182–183) for I.I.T. appears to be the most interesting in the wide range of buildings planned for this campus. It is the first I.I.T. building without brick, being entirely of glass and steel. Here again structural elements are revealed with decorative effect; all supporting members are placed outside the volume of the building.

Among the projects with which Mies has been concerned is a row house (pages 178–179) whose columns, like those of the Farnsworth house, are welded to floor and roof fascias. However, in the row house the columns do not touch the ground but are joined to the steel fascia of the floor slab, which supports them. The steel wall frames are prefabricated and, together with the structural system, suggests one possible method of mass produced houses.

Mies, in his 1950 address to the I.I.T. (see bibl. 94) has said, "Wherever technology reaches its real fulfillment, it transcends into architecture. It is true that architecture depends on facts, but its real field of activity is in the realm of significance." It is Mies's particular genius in the exploitation of technological significance which leads to his architectural innovations. This is well illustrated in the fascinating experiment in framing projected for a 50-foot square house (pages 180–181). The roof of this house is composed of steel egg-crating welded to a steel sheet above. The increase in strength and rigidity and even distribution of stresses, which such a system provides, enables Mies to support the

roof with a single column placed in the exact center of each façade—
there are no supports at the corners. The walls of this house are entirely
of glass butt-joined at the corners to avoid additional steel framing.
Since the volume of the house is no longer defined by corner accents,
the effect is that of a space without axis, a building composed totally of
corners. No ceiling plane covers the roof framing; the steel egg-crate
itself creates a rich, coffered ceiling. The "fifty-by-fifty" house is the
most radical of Mies's efforts over the past thirty years to simplify, ar-
ticulate, and give artistic expression to structural system.

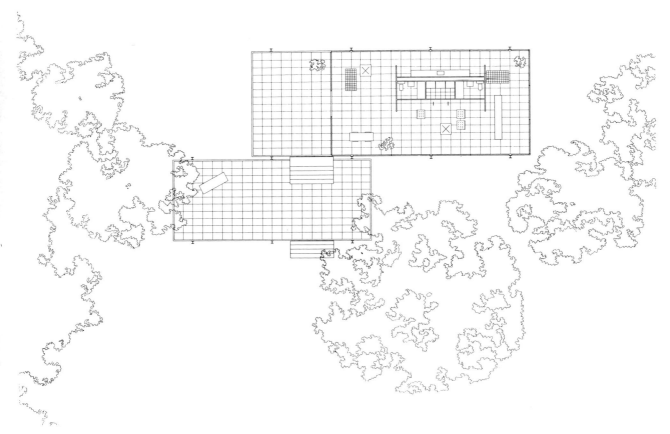

Farnsworth House. Plan

House for Dr. Edith Farnsworth, Plano, Illinois. 1950. Glass and steel

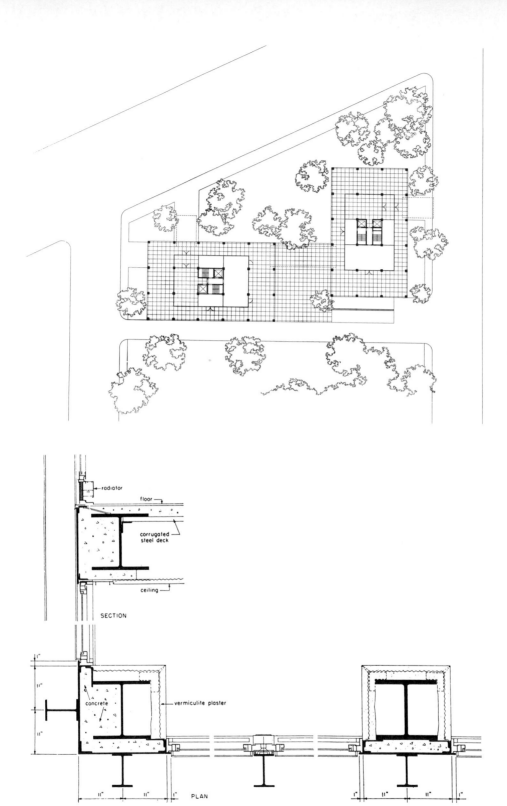

Apartment Houses at 860 Lake Shore Drive. Plan and sections

Apartment Houses at 860 Lake Shore Drive, Chicago. 1951. Pace Associates, and Holsman, Holsman, Klekamp and Taylor, Associated

Apartment Houses at 860 Lake Shore Drive. Connecting passage

Apartment Houses at 860 Lake Shore Drive. Lobby

Chapel, I.I.T., Chicago. 1952

Staircase of Arts Club of Chicago. 1951

Row house. Prototype wall

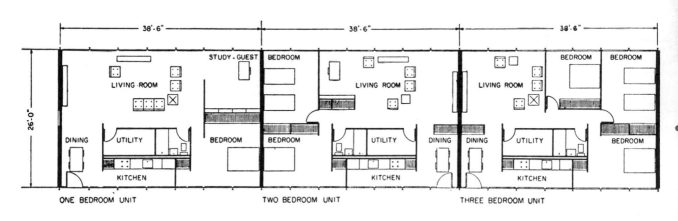

Row house. 1951. Plan

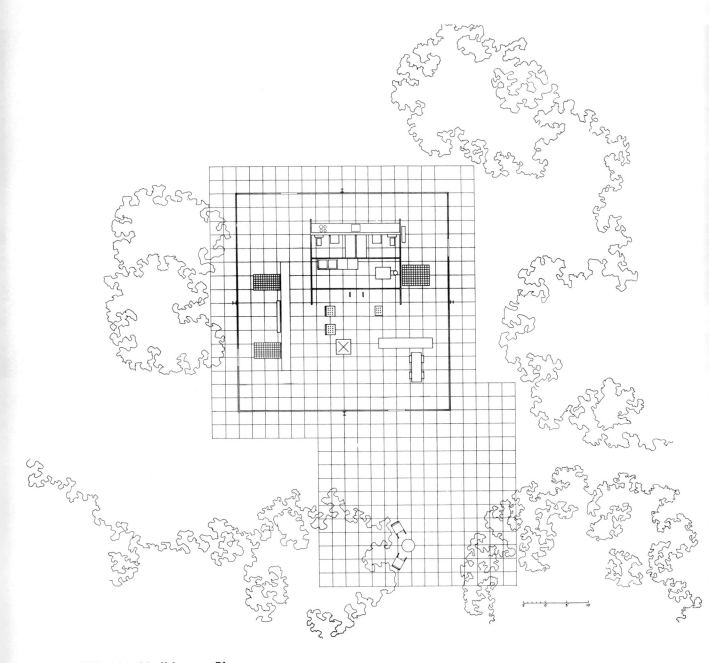

"Fifty-by-fifty" house. Plan

Project: "Fifty-by-fifty" house. 1951

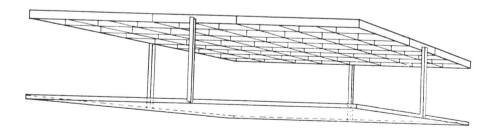

Roof detail

Project: Architecture and Design Building, I.I.T., Chicago. 1952. Model

Architecture and Design Building, I.I.T., Chicago. Model

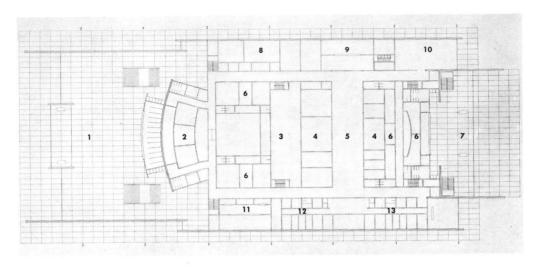

Ground floor

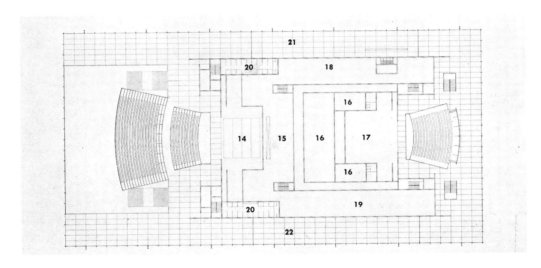

First floor

1. Entrance to large auditorium
2. Orchestra rehearsal and instrument storage
3. Costume storage
4. Rehearsal rooms
5. Lounge
6. Dressing rooms for the artists
7. Entrance hall to the small auditorium

8. Costume workshops
9. Cafeteria and kitchen
10. Delivery and garage
11. Business offices
12. Technical and design studios
13. Administration
14. Main stage, large auditorium
15. Back stage

16. Paint shops
17. Main stage, small auditorium
18. Scenery workshop
19. Storage
20. Dressing rooms for soloists
21. Theater restaurant
22. Promenade

Project: National Theater, Mannheim, Germany. 1953. Model

185

WRITINGS BY MIES VAN DER ROHE

1922: TWO GLASS SKYSCRAPERS

Illustrations, pages 23-29; text, page 22.

Skyscrapers reveal their bold structural pattern during construction. Only then does the gigantic steel web seem impressive. When the outer walls are put in place, the structural system which is the basis of all artistic design, is hidden by a chaos of meaningless and trivial forms. When finished, these buildings are impressive only because of their size; yet they could surely be more than mere examples of our technical ability. Instead of trying to solve the new problems with old forms, we should develop the new forms from the very nature of the new problems.

We can see the new structural principles most clearly when we use glass in place of the outer walls, which is feasible today since in a skeleton building these outer walls do not actually carry weight. The use of glass imposes new solutions.

In my project for a skyscraper at the Friedrichstrasse Station in Berlin [page 24] I used a prismatic form which seemed to me to fit best the triangular site of the building. I placed the glass walls at slight angles to each other to avoid the monotony of over-large glass surfaces.

I discovered by working with actual glass models that the important thing is the play of reflections and not the effect of light and shadow as in ordinary buildings.

The results of these experiments can be seen in the second scheme published here [page 28]. At first glance the curved outline of the plan seems arbitrary. These curves, however, were determined by three factors: sufficient illumination of the interior, the massing of the building viewed from the street, and lastly the play of reflections. I proved in the glass model that calculations of light and shadow do not help in designing an all-glass building.

The only fixed points of the plan are the stair and elevator shafts. All the other elements of the plan fit the needs of the building and are designed to be carried out in glass.

From *Frühlicht*, (bibl. 1)

1923: THE OFFICE BUILDING

Illustration, page 31; text, pages 26, 30.

The office building is a house of work, of organization, of clarity, of economy.

Broad, light workspace, unbroken, but articulated according to the organization of the work. Maximum effect with minimum means.

The materials: concrete, steel, glass.

Reinforced concrete structures are skeletons by nature. No gingerbread. No fortress. Columns and girders eliminate bearing walls. This is skin and bone construction.

Functional division of the workspace determines the width of the building: 16 meters. The most economic system was found to be two rows of columns spanning 8 meters with 4 meters cantilevered on either side. The girders are spaced 5 meters apart. These girders carry the floor slabs, which at the end of the cantilevers are turned up perpendicularly to form the outer skin of the building. Cabinets are placed against these walls in order to permit free visibility in the center of the rooms. Above the cabinets, which are 2 meters high, runs a continuous band of windows.

From G, No. 1 (bibl. 2)

1923: APHORISMS ON ARCHITECTURE AND FORM

We reject all esthetic speculation, all doctrine, all formalism.
Architecture is the will of an epoch translated into space; living, changing, new.
Not yesterday, not tomorrow, only today can be given form.
Only this kind of building will be creative.

Create form out of the nature of our tasks with the methods of
our time.
This is our task.

From G, No. 1 (bibl. 2)

We refuse to recognize problems of form, but only problems
of building.
Form is not the aim of our work, but only the result.
Form, by itself, does not exist.
Form as an aim is formalism; and that we reject.

From G, No. 2 (bibl. 27)

Essentially our task is to free the practice of building from the control
of esthetic speculators and restore it to what it should exclusively be:
building.

From G, (bibl. 27)

1924: THE INDUSTRIALIZATION OF BUILDING METHODS

Our building methods today must be industrialized. Although everyone concerned has opposed this until recently, it is now being discussed
even outside the building trades. This seems like progress, even though
few are yet really convinced.

Industrialization, which is advancing in all fields today, would long ago
have overtaken the building trades, in spite of their obsolete thinking, if
there had not been special obstacles. I consider the industrialization of
building methods the key problem of the day for architects and builders. Once we succeed in this, our social, economic, technical and even
artistic problems will be easy to solve. How can industrialization be carried out? The question can be answered if we consider what has thus far

prevented it. Outmoded building methods are not to blame; they are the result rather than the cause.

There have been many attempts to find new building methods which have succeeded only in those branches of the industry in which industrialization was possible. The potentialities of assembly methods in building have also been exaggerated; they are in use only in factory and barn construction. The steel industry pioneered the manufacture of fabricated parts ready for assembly, and today the lumber industry is trying the same thing. In all other building, however, the roughwork and most of the interior fittings are carried out in the traditional way—by hand work. Hand work cannot be eliminated by changes in organization of the building industry, nor by improving work methods, for it is just this hand work that keeps small contractors going. It has been demonstrated that the use of larger masonry blocks can lower material and labor costs, but this in no way eliminates hand labor. Besides, the old brick masonry has many advantages over these newer methods. The problem before us is not the rationalization of the present methods, but rather a revolution in the whole nature of the building industry. The nature of the building process will not change as long as we employ essentially the same building materials, for they require hand labor.

Industrialization of the processes of construction is a question of materials. Our first consideration, therefore, must be to find a new building material. Our technologists must and will succeed in inventing a material which can be industrially manufactured and processed and which will be weatherproof, soundproof and insulating. It must be a light material which not only permits but requires industrial production. All the parts will be made in a factory and the work at the site will consist only of assemblage, requiring extremely few man-hours. This will greatly reduce building costs. Then the new architecture will come into its own. I am convinced that traditional methods of construction will disappear. In case anyone regrets that the house of the future can no longer be made by hand workers, it should be borne in mind that the automobile is no longer manufactured by carriage-makers.

From G, No. 3 (bibl. 4)

1924: ARCHITECTURE AND THE TIMES

Greek temples, Roman basilicas and medieval cathedrals are significant to us as creations of a whole epoch rather than as works of individual architects. Who asks for the names of these builders? Of what significance are the fortuitous personalities of their creators? Such buildings are impersonal by their very nature. They are pure expressions of their time. Their true meaning is that they are symbols of their epoch.

Architecture is the will of the epoch translated into space. Until this simple truth is clearly recognized, the new architecture will be uncertain and tentative. Until then it must remain a chaos of undirected forces. The question as to the nature of architecture is of decisive importance. It must be understood that all architecture is bound up with its own time, that it can only be manifested in living tasks and in the medium of its epoch. In no age has it been otherwise.

It is hopeless to try to use the forms of the past in our architecture. Even the strongest artistic talent must fail in this attempt. Again and again we see talented architects who fall short because their work is not in tune with their age. In the last analysis, in spite of their great gifts, they are dilettantes; for it makes no difference how enthusiastically they do the wrong thing. It is a question of essentials. It is not possible to move forward and look backwards; he who lives in the past cannot advance.

The whole trend of our time is toward the secular. The endeavors of the mystics will be remembered as mere episodes. Despite our greater understanding of life, we shall build no cathedrals. Nor do the brave gestures of the Romantics mean anything to us, for behind them we detect their empty form. Ours is not an age of pathos; we do not respect flights of the spirit as much as we value reason and realism.

The demand of our time for realism and functionalism must be met. Only then will our buildings express the potential greatness of our time; and only a fool can say that it has no greatness.

We are concerned today with questions of a general nature. The individual is losing significance; his destiny is no longer what interests us. The decisive achievements in all fields are impersonal and their authors are for the most part unknown. They are part of the trend of our time toward anonymity. Our engineering structures are examples. **Gigantic** dams, great industrial installations and huge bridges are built as a matter of course, with no designer's name attached to them. They point to the technology of the future.

If we compare the mammoth heaviness of Roman aqueducts with the web-like lightness of modern cranes or massive vaulting with thin reinforced concrete construction, we realize how much our architecture differs from that of the past in form and expression. Modern industrial methods have had a great influence on this development. It is meaningless to object that modern buildings are only utilitarian.

If we discard all romantic conceptions, we can recognize the stone structures of the Greeks, the brick and concrete construction of the Romans and the medieval cathedrals, all as bold engineering achievements. It can be taken for granted that the first Gothic buildings were viewed as intruders in their Romanesque surroundings.

Our utilitarian buildings can become worthy of the name of architecture only if they truly interpret their time by their perfect functional expression.

From *Der Querschnitt* (bibl. 3)

1927: A LETTER ON FORM IN ARCHITECTURE

Dear Dr. Riezler:

My attack is not against form, but against form as an *end in itself*.

I make this attack because of what I have learned.

Form as an end inevitably results in mere formalism.

This effort is directed only to the exterior. But only what has life on the inside has a living exterior.

Only what has intensity of life can have intensity of form.

Every "how" is based on a "what."

The un-formed is no worse than the over-formed.

The former is nothing; the latter is mere appearance.

Real form presupposes real life.

But no "has been" or "would be."

This is our criterion:

We should judge not so much by the results as by the creative process.

For it is just this that reveals whether the form is derived from life or invented for its own sake.

That is why the creative process is so essential.

Life is what is decisive for us.

In all its plenitude and in its spiritual and material relations.

Is it not one of the most important tasks of the Werkbund to clarify, analyze and order our spiritual and material situation and thus to take the lead?

Must not all else be left to the forces of creation?

From Die Form (bibl. 7)

1927: POLICY OF THE STUTTGART EXPOSITION

Foreword to the official catalog of the Werkbund Exposition *Weissenhofsiedlung* at Stuttgart, of which Mies was the Director. Illustrations, pages 44-45; text page 49.

The problem of the modern dwelling is primarily architectural, in spite of its technical and economic aspects. It is a complex problem of planning and can therefore be solved only by creative minds, not by calculation or organization. Therefore, I felt it imperative, in spite of current talk about "rationalization" and "standardization," to keep the project at Stuttgart from being one-sided or doctrinaire. I have therefore invited leading representatives of the modern movement to make their contributions to the problem of the modern dwelling.

I have refrained from laying down a rigid program in order to leave each individual as free as possible to carry out his ideas. In drawing up the general plan I felt it important to avoid regulations that might interfere with free expression.

From Bau und Wohnung (bibl. 9)

1927: THE DESIGN OF APARTMENT HOUSES

A note on the design of Mies's own apartment building. Illustrations, pages 46-48; text, page 42.

Today the factor of economy makes rationalization and standardization imperative for rental housing. On the other hand, the increased complexity of our requirements demands flexibility. The future will have to reckon with both. For this purpose skeleton construction is the most suitable system. It makes possible rationalized building methods and allows the interior to be freely divided. If we regard kitchens and bathrooms, because of their plumbing, as a fixed core, then all other space may be partitioned by means of movable walls. This should, I believe, satisfy all normal requirements.

From *Bau und Wohnung* (bibl. 10)

1928: EXPOSITIONS

Expositions are implements for industry and culture. They should be used as such.

The effectiveness of an exposition depends on its approach to basic problems. The history of great expositions shows us that only expositions which treat living problems are successful.

The era of monumental expositions that make money is past. Today we judge an exposition by what it accomplishes in the cultural field.

Economic, technical and cultural conditions have changed radically. Both technology and industry face entirely new problems. It is very important for our culture and our society, as well as for technology and industry, to find good solutions.

German industry—and indeed European industry as a whole—must understand and solve these specific tasks. The path must lead from quantity towards quality—from the extensive to the intensive.

Along this path industry and technology will join with the forces of thought and culture.

We are in a period of transition—a transition that will change the world.

To explain and help along this transition will be the responsiblity of future expositions, and they will be successful only in so far as they concentrate on this task and treat the central problem of our time—the intensification of our life.

From *Die Form* (bibl. 11)

1930: THE NEW ERA

Speech delivered at a Werkbund meeting in Vienna.

The new era is a fact: it exists, irrespective of our "yes" or "no." Yet it is neither better nor worse than any other era. It is pure datum, in itself without value content. Therefore I will not try to define it or clarify its basic structure.

Let us not give undue importance to mechanization and standardization.

Let us accept changed economic and social conditions as a fact.

All these take their blind and fateful course.

One thing will be decisive: the way we assert ourselves in the face of circumstance.

Here the problems of the spirit begin. The important question to ask is not "what" but "how." What goods we produce or what tools we use are not questions of spiritual value.

How the question of skyscrapers versus low buildings is settled, whether we build of steel and glass, are unimportant questions from the point of view of spirit.

Whether we tend to centralization or decentralization in city planning is a practical question, not a question of value.

Yet it is just the question of value that is decisive.

We must set up new values, fix our ultimate goals so that we may establish standards.

For what is right and significant for any era—including the new era—is this: to give the spirit the opportunity for existence.

From *Die Form* (bibl. 13)

1930: ART CRITICISM

An impromptu speech delivered at a symposium, "Artists Discuss the Critics."

Are not mistakes in judgment natural? For is criticism so easy? Is not true criticism as rare as art? I would like, therefore, to call your attention to the essential nature of criticism, including art criticism. For unless this is clear, there can be no true criticism and demands will be made that critics cannot answer.

The rôle of the critic is to test a work of art from the point of view of significance and value. To do this, however, the critic must first understand the work of art. This is not easy. Works of art have a life of their own; they are not accessible to every one. If they are to have meaning for us we must approach them on their own terms. That is, at the same time, the opportunity and the limitation of criticism.

Another limitation of criticism is the hierarchy of values, without which there can be no real measurement. True criticism must always serve a set of values.

From *Das Kunstblatt* (bibl. 12)

1938: INAUGURAL ADDRESS AS DIRECTOR OF ARCHITECTURE AT ARMOUR INSTITUTE OF TECHNOLOGY

All education must begin with the practical side of life.

Real education, however, must transcend this to mould the personality.

The first aim should be to equip the student with the knowledge and skill for practical life.

The second aim should be to develop his personality and to enable him to make the right use of this knowledge and skill.

Thus true education is concerned not only with practical goals but also with values.

196

By our practical aims we are bound to the specific structure of our epoch. Our values, on the other hand, are rooted in the spiritual nature of men.

Our practical aims measure only our material progress. The values we profess reveal the level of our culture.

Different as practical aims and values are, they are nevertheless closely connected.

For to what else should our values be related if not to our aims in life?

Human existence is predicated on the two spheres together. Our aims assure us of our material life, our values make possible our spiritual life.

If this is true of all human activity where even the slightest question of value is involved, how especially is it true of the sphere of architecture.

In its simplest form architecture is rooted in entirely functional considerations, but it can reach up through all degrees of value to the highest sphere of spiritual existence, into the realm of pure art.

In organizing an architectural education system we must recognize this situation if we are to succeed in our efforts. We must fit the system to this reality. Any teaching of architecture must explain these relations and interrelations.

We must make clear, step by step, what things are possible, necessary and significant.

If teaching has any purpose, it is to implant true insight and responsibility.

Education must lead us from irresponsible opinion to true responsible judgment.

It must lead us from chance and arbitrariness to rational clarity and intellectual order.

Therefore let us guide our students over the road of discipline from materials, through function, to creative work. Let us lead them into the healthy world of primitive building methods, where there was meaning in every stroke of an axe, expression in every bite of a chisel.

Where can we find greater structural clarity than in the wooden buildings of old? Where else can we find such unity of material, construction and form?

Here the wisdom of whole generations is stored.

What feeling for material and what power of expression there is in these buildings!

What warmth and beauty they have! They seem to be echoes of old songs.

And buildings of stone as well: what natural feeling they express!

What a clear understanding of the material! How surely it is joined!

What sense they had of where stone could and could not be used!

Where do we find such wealth of structure? Where more natural and healthy beauty?

How easily they laid beamed ceilings on those old stone walls and with what sensitive feeling they cut doorways through them!

What better examples could there be for young architects? Where else could they learn such simple and true crafts than from these unknown masters?

We can also learn from brick.

How sensible is this small handy shape, so useful for every purpose! What logic in its bonding, pattern and texture!

What richness in the simplest wall surface! But what discipline this material imposes!

Thus each material has its specific characteristics which we must understand if we want to use it.

This is no less true of steel and concrete. We must remember that everything depends on how we use a material, not on the material itself.

Also new materials are not necessarily superior. Each material is only what we make it.

We must be as familiar with the functions of our buildings as with our materials. We must analyze them and clarify them. We must learn, for example, what distinguishes a building to live in from other kinds of building.

We must learn what a building can be, what it should be, and also what it must not be.

We shall examine one by one every function of a building and use it as a basis for form.

Just as we acquainted ourselves with materials and just as we must understand functions, we must become familiar with the psychological and spiritual factors of our day.

No cultural activity is possible otherwise; for we are dependent on the spirit of our time.

Therefore we must understand the motives and forces of our time and analyze their structure from three points of view: the material, the functional and the spiritual.

We must make clear in what respects our epoch differs from others and in what respects it is similar.

At this point the problem of technology of construction arises.

We shall be concerned with genuine problems—problems related to the value and purpose of our technology.

We shall show that technology not only promises greatness and power, but also involves dangers; that good and evil apply to it as to all human actions; that it is our task to make the right decision.

Every decision leads to a special kind of order.

Therefore we must make clear what principles of order are possible and clarify them.

Let us recognize that the mechanistic principle of order overemphasizes the materialistic and functionalistic factors in life, since it fails to satisfy our feeling that means must be subsidiary to ends and our desire for dignity and value.

The idealistic principle of order, however, with its over-emphasis on the ideal and the formal, satisfies neither our interest in simple reality nor our practical sense.

So we shall emphasize the organic principle of order as a means of achieving the successful relationship of the parts to each other and to the whole.

And here we shall take our stand.

The long path from material through function to creative work has only a single goal: to create order out of the desperate confusion of our time.

We must have order, allocating to each thing its proper place and giving to each thing its due according to its nature.

We would do this so perfectly that the world of our creations will blossom from within.

We want no more; we can do no more.

Nothing can express the aim and meaning of our work better than the profound words of St. Augustine: "Beauty is the splendor of Truth."

1940: FRANK LLOYD WRIGHT

An appreciation written for the unpublished catalog of the Frank Lloyd Wright Exhibition held at the Museum of Modern Art.

About the beginning of this century the great European artistic restoration instigated by William Morris, having grown over-refined, gradually began to lose force. Distinct signs of exhaustion became manifest. The attempt to revive architecture from the point of view of form appeared to be doomed. The lack of a valid convention became apparent, and even the greatest efforts of the artists of the day did not succeed in overcoming this deficiency. Their efforts, however, were restricted to the subjective. Since the authentic approach to architecture should always be the objective, we find the only valid solutions of that time to be in those cases where objective limits were imposed and there was no opportunity for subjective license. This was true of the field of industrial building. It is enough to remember the significant creations of Peter Behrens for the electrical industry [page 11]. But in all other problems of architectural creation the architect ventured into the dangerous realm of the historical. To some of these men a revival of Classic forms seemed reasonable, and in the field of monumental architecture, even imperative.

Of course this was not true of all early twentieth-century architects, particularly not of Van de Velde and Berlage [pages 10 and 16]. Both remained steadfast in their ideals. To the former, any deviation from a way of thinking once acknowledged to be necessary was impossible because of his intellectual integrity; to the latter, because of his almost religious faith in his ideals and the sincerity of his character. For these reasons the one received our highest respect and admiration, the other, our special veneration and love.

Nevertheless we young architects found ourselves in painful inner discord. Our enthusiastic hearts demanded the unqualified, and we were ready to pledge ourselves to an idea. But the potential vitality of the architectural idea of the period had by that time been lost.

This then was approximately the situation in 1910.

At this moment, so critical for us, the exhibition of the work of Frank Lloyd Wright came to Berlin. This comprehensive display and the exhaustive publication of his works enabled us to become really acquainted with the achievements of this architect. The encounter was destined to prove of great significance to the European development.

The work of this great master presented an architectural world of unexpected force, clarity of language and disconcerting richness of form. Here, finally, was a master-builder drawing upon the veritable fountainhead of architecture; who with true originality lifted his creations into the light. Here again, at long last, genuine organic architecture flowered. The more we were absorbed in the study of these creations, the greater became our admiration for his incomparable talent, the boldness of his conceptions and the independence of his thought and action. The dynamic impulse emanating from his work invigorated a whole generation. His influence was strongly felt even when it was not actually visible.

So after this first encounter we followed the development of this rare man with wakeful hearts. We watched with astonishment the exuberant unfolding of the gifts of one who had been endowed by nature with the most splendid talents. In his undiminishing power he resembles a giant tree in a wide landscape, which year after year, attains a more noble crown.

1943: A MUSEUM FOR A SMALL CITY

Illustrations, pages 161-164; text, pages 154, 156.

The museum for a small city should not emulate its metropolitan counter parts. The value of such a museum depends upon the quality of its works of art and the manner in which they are exhibited.

The first problem is to establish the museum as a center for the enjoyment, not the interment of art. In this project the barrier between the work of art and the living community is erased by a garden approach for the display of sculpture. Sculpture placed inside the building enjoys an equal spatial freedom, because the open plan permits it to be seen against the surrounding hills. The architectural space thus achieved becomes a defining rather than a confining space. A work such as Picasso's *Guernica* [page 162] has been difficult to place in the usual museum gallery. Here it can be shown to greatest advantage and become an element in space against a changing background.

The building, conceived as one large area, allows complete flexibility. The type of structure which permits this is the steel frame. This construction permits the erection of a building with only three basic elements—a floor slab, columns and a roof plate. The floor and paved terraces would be of stone.

Under the same roof, but separated from the exhibit space, would be the offices of administration. These would have their own toilet and storage facilities in a basement under the office area.

Small pictures would be exhibited on free-standing walls. The entire building space would be available for larger groups, encouraging a more representative use of the museum than is customary today, and creating a noble background for the civic and cultural life of the whole community.

From *Architectural Forum* (bibl. 65)

1950: ADDRESS TO ILLINOIS INSTITUTE OF TECHNOLOGY

Technology is rooted in the past.
It dominates the present and tends into the future.
It is a real historical movement—
one of the great movements which shape and
represent their epoch.
It can be compared only with the Classic
discovery of man as a person,
the Roman will to power,
and the religious movement of the Middle Ages.
Technology is far more than a method,
it is a world in itself.
As a method it is superior in almost every respect.
But only where it is left to itself as in
gigantic structures of engineering, there
technology reveals its true nature.
There it is evident that it is not only a useful means,
that it is something, something in itself,
something that has a meaning and a powerful form—
so powerful in fact, that it is not easy to name it.
Is that still technology or is it architecture?
And that may be the reason why some people
are convinced that architecture will be outmoded
and replaced by technology.
Such a conviction is not based on clear thinking.
The opposite happens.
Wherever technology reaches its real fulfillment,
it transcends into architecture.
It is true that architecture depends on facts,
but its real field of activity is in the realm
of significance.
I hope you will understand that architecture
has nothing to do with the inventions of forms.

It is not a playground for children, young or old.
Architecture is the real battleground of the spirit.
Architecture wrote the history of the epochs
and gave them their names.
Architecture depends on its time.
It is the crystallization of its inner structure,
the slow unfolding of its form.
That is the reason why technology and architecture
are so closely related.
Our real hope is that they grow together,
that someday the one be the expression of
the other.
Only then will we have an architecture worthy
of its name:
Architecture as a true symbol of our time.

EPILOGUE: THIRTY YEARS AFTER

The following discussion took place in December 1977, when Philip Johnson was consulted about the present reissue of his monograph on Mies van der Rohe. Participants in the discussion with Mr. Johnson were Ludwig Glaeser, Curator of the Mies van der Rohe Archive at The Museum of Modern Art, and Arthur Drexler, Director of the Department of Architecture and Design at the same institution.

L. G.   What did you know about Mies before you met him?

P. J.   I first learned of Mies through Gustav Platz's *Baukunst der neuesten Zeit.* It must have been in 1930 because I had already met Russell [Henry-Russell Hitchcock], and this was the first book on modern architecture you could refer to. It had pictures of his early work and included the Barcelona Pavilion. To me he was a greater architect than Le Corbusier or Oud, the people Hitchcock liked best. I thought this was the new Gospel, and he fit well enough in the Gospel preached by Hitchcock and [Alfred] Barr. I recognized we could all hang out with this one, so I insisted on going to see him, and on seeing some of the apartments he'd done in Berlin. I was traveling around Germany with John McAndrew.

A. D.   You felt he was a better architect than Le Corbusier or Oud even before you saw the actual buildings?

P. J.   Yes. They seemed less factorylike, more classical; the Barcelona Pavilion had marble, and the Schinkel-Persius thing was already in my mind. I don't know why. I tried to convert Hitchcock to Mies and I showed him an apartment. I remember there was a Barcelona chair in canary yellow leather, and he said "Well, I don't know what you are talking about. That's not my dish of tea." And I couldn't imagine what was wrong with Hitchcock. I knew I was right.

L. G.   You must have almost settled in Berlin in 1930, you even had stationery printed.

P. J.   I had stationery printed, as I was preparing the book, and lived at Achenbach str. 22, it's no longer there.

L. G.   Did you see Mies frequently that summer?

P. J.   No, it was the next summer I saw more of him, in 1931.

L. G.   During the Berlin Building Exhibition?

P. J.   Yes, the *Bau-Ausstellung*—that year [1931] I saw him most. He loved to drive in the country. The only way I could get to see him was to invite him for a drive. Nobody had cars in Germany in 1931, and I had a Cord, naturally. One remembers these things . . . more vividly. His favorite buildings were the *Hallenkirchen* [churches with naves of equal height], up north toward Stettin, toward Lübeck.

L. G.   *Backsteingotik* [brick Gothic].

P. J.   That was where he felt most at home: in the *Hallen,* the tall churches. I didn't understand German Gothic. I was brought up on Île de France Gothic. It was a little strange, the tall halls done in brick. I used to try to get him to talk about Schinkel. But he would say yes if I got enthusiastic and he would never really discuss it, even though he did that early thing that looks like the Persius house. When I first found that I jumped for joy and said "Oh, you know Persius?" He didn't, at least not by name. It was hard to know what Mies had seen and what not. The other thing he liked to do was drink and eat. Of course they had very good food. We used to go to Schlichter's all the time and I'd pay for him. It was frightfully expensive and he had no means of support that I could see. In 1930 he had only my apartment to do. He did it as if it were six skyscrapers— the amount of work he put into that apartment was incredible.

L. G.   According to one of Mies's collaborators from these years, you actually occupied a drafting table in his office and, as he claims, got from him some drafting instructions.

P. J.   No, I can't remember ever having occupied a drafting table there, but I was around and may have picked up some tricks of the trade.

A. D.   Did you know Lilly Reich?

P. J.   I met her through Mies. She was very jealous. She could see that he and I could talk about things, but I was draining this man of his precious hours with Lilly. She was a very unpleasant

206

woman, no sense of humor at all. Sometimes she went on these rides with us in 1931, but very seldom.

A. D.   What was your impression of how much of the furniture she was doing?

P. J.   He did everything.

L. G.   There is in the Archive evidence to the contrary.

P. J.   I felt that he did all the design at the *Bau-Ausstellung.* The white room she may have done, because Mies never really got into furnishings in spite of the amount he talked about it, and I don't blame him. Of course you have to realize the incredible competence of the German craftsmen. They were all starving. Everybody was so hungry that I could get the greatest craftsmen in the world to do a little suitcase for the camera I bought there.

L. G.   I know. The Mies Archive has all the correspondence on your apartment, including the cabinetmaker's invoices.

P. J.   Mies liked the plan for that apartment. He said, "That's an extraordinary plan, did you do it?" I said, "Heavens no. That's an American commercial dwelling." There wasn't a wasted inch, unlike European apartments, all taken up with corridors and high ceilings. He thought that was incredible, how you could get exposures and how you didn't mind walking through rooms. One thing he was absolutely no good at was lighting. He just wouldn't focus on it—look at those fixtures in the Tugendhat house.

A. D.   In the photographs reproduced in your book, as well as those used by everyone else, the burn spots created by the lighting are always airbrushed out.

P. J.   Yes, and the Tugendhat house was the worst of all.

L. G.   I think Mies had worse problems with lighting than most of the other modern architects. Perhaps because of his northern-German background . . .

P. J.   Cloudy, you mean?

L. G.   Like the Dutch. There's no curtain in front of any Dutch living room. They like the cloud spectacle, as they hate to lose a sun ray.

P. J.   With Mies it was very hard to find any of his precedents because everything sprang, of course, originally from his mind. There weren't any precedents for architecture in those days.

A. D.   You confirmed his opinion?

P. J. I went right along with him. I was young and didn't have any more sense. The only man he mentioned was Berlage. He never mentioned Behrens.

L. G. Berlage was probably safest because, although he knew him well personally, the relationship was not too direct. I once went on a probing trip on Japanese influences, but he evaded the issue and instead told me about everything he admired in medieval architecture. Similarly with Schinkel. I always assumed, just from looking over Mies's work, that he knew his Schinkel very well. What I tried to find out was whether he had absorbed it directly or through Behrens. It is known that Behrens used to take the entire office on weekend tours to Schinkel monuments in Berlin and environs.

P. J. I didn't know that.

L. G. And of course, the Behrens buildings from the years Mies was in his office were almost copies of Schinkel precedents—the Mannesmann Building of the Schauspielhaus, the Petersburg Embassy of the Altes Museum, and so on.

P. J. And yet it's funny, when we used to go around Berlin, he never used to say "that's good, that's secondary." He would never make decisions the way historians, or us mixed historians would do, never would ask where Schinkel was being the most Schinkel. That wasn't of interest to him.

L. G. When you could get him to talk, did he talk about his daily or his past life—didn't he like to tell anecdotes, or did he always stick to architecture?

P. J. I was never interested in anything else. I didn't even know he was married.

L. G. So his personal life never surfaced?

P. J. No. Even in philosophy, which he purported to be interested in, he never digressed from Aquinas.

L. G. Did you ever observe him talking to students or associates?

P. J. Yes, they resented the fact that he didn't—in Chicago, of course.

L. G. What was Mies's reaction to your book in 1947? It was, after all, the first monograph on his work.

P. J. He was conscious of what I put in, in the way of pictures. He didn't let me publish the sketch of the interior of the Neue Wache [New Guard House] for the war memorial competition. He said it wasn't enough of a statement. But he never read the text—at least that was what he said. "I can't stand to read anything about myself." And yet, of the things he did write himself, what lapidary precision and clarity.

L. G.   He must have labored hard, to judge from the drafts. It's as if it were to be carved in stone, the ancestral occupation; and to be worth the effort, it had to be lapidary.

A. D.   How did you think of his book when you wrote it? What did you intend it to do?

P. J.   I thought of it as hagiography, exegesis, propaganda—I just wanted to show that Mies was the greatest architect in the world.

A. D.   The text is still quite persuasive, but one of its characteristics is that you treat the buildings as if they were of equal importance. Did you really think that was the case?

P. J.   No, of course not. I didn't know what to make of the Reichsbank project. It was so mundane, so symmetrical, and I didn't like the way he used the banking room as the base, fitting it on to the building. I didn't know what to say about it, so I followed the example of Russell: don't mention what you don't like. The Wolf, Lange, and Krefeld houses I hated, mostly because I didn't like holes in brick walls and didn't think Mies did that best.

A. D.   You presented the I.I.T. buildings as if they were the inevitable development of Miesian logic, and you also related them to the Chicago tradition. But actually such buildings were already being done in Germany with very similar detailing.

L. G.   Steel frames with glass and brick infill. You collected one example for the 1932 exhibition—Theodor Merrill's Königsgrube coal mine building. I found another one from another architect, Fritz Schupp, who was actually known here. *Architectural Forum* published in 1930 a summary of his book *Architekt und Ingenieur*.

P. J.   Right. I don't think there is any question about Mies's use of vernacular factory style; but it's interesting that his factories weren't like Albert Kahn's, they were German vernacular.

L. G.   I think it all goes back to late nineteenth-century anonymous Industrial structures, and as you say, it is basically a translation into steel of the vernacular *Fachwerkbauten*.

P. J.   Timber-frame buildings—Mies always had those old barns lying around his house, but the German vernacular is different. In this country we tend to do the most logical thing in the world, which is to build the skeleton and then pay no attention to it—you put the skin over it. So you end up with Kahn's endless strips, whereas the Merrill thing, based on a frame, was perhaps derived from wood *Fachwerk*. But it didn't bother the Germans. It didn't strike them that carrying the skin independent of the frame would be so much cheaper. I did a factory for the de Menil's in Houston, which they didn't build, and in imitation of Mies I had an expression of both the beams and the columns. The practical builders were horrified. They said, "Don't you know, you dog—young and enthusiastic—that it is so expensive to stop everything when you get to a column. Windows must never stop, because one thing that a window has is its own life, and your columns have another life, so you keep them separate." But *Fachwerk* to the Germans was as natural as eating. I didn't mention it because I didn't know it.

A.D. It's an interesting point because without that in the back of one's mind, one sees I.I.T. as high art classicizing, or as Japanese. Its origin in German vernacular is harder to grasp.

L. G. I suspect Mies also chose the factory building as a model because he thought it was appropriate for an Institute of Technology in a period of wartime austerity.

P. J. Well, I think he then translated that into his mysticism of steel, which he felt was a new thing. I showed him that Merrill factory. He was horrified by its romanticism. We admire now the fact that Merrill could break it down into several boxes. As I remember, it was quite in and out—and that doesn't fit either economy, which was Mies's key word, or natural steel construction. Much better to build an absolute shape and then shove everything in.

A.D. How about the first project for the *Weissenhofsiedlung*? You described it in one sentence without any discussion at all. Even though the composition seems different from anything Mies did before or after, it looks quite beautiful.

P. J. Well, actually I *was* fascinated by Italian villages, but I wouldn't admit it.

A.D. How would you do the book today?

P. J. I didn't discuss the influence of Cubism, and the connections with Expressionism were a mystery to me. Those are two things I would go into now. The *de Stijl* influence is clear enough—in fact he did it better than de Stijl ever did. Alfred [Barr] insisted on emphasizing the glass skyscrapers, which he thought were beautiful, and I wouldn't change that. I didn't really like

Mies's *Weissenhofsiedlung* apartment house—one side of it looked like a factory. I think I might treat his courthouse project for himself a little differently; it really had a terrible plan. Most of all I would look into Expressionism, into the feeling of defeated Berlin, the character of the *Novembergruppe,* the suddenness with which Mies went from what he had been doing to the glass skyscraper of 1921.

L. G.   As you know, in the early 1920s he destroyed most of the drawings done just before and just after the war.

A. D.   What buildings do you think of now as the most important?

P. J.   The European work is hard to evaluate that way because I think I would do a complete retake on the years 1919 to 1929. Of course the Barcelona Pavilion is the masterpiece, even though it never had as much influence as his later work. Of the American work, the first plan for I.I.T., a kind of successor to the Alexanderplatz, which I loved; the Convention Hall project; and the Farnsworth house. And one would have to have a separate category for details—the corner and the mullion. Whatever you choose, it involves an idea. I think that's what Mies is about. He made history with his ideas.

BRIEF CHRONOLOGY

1886	Born March 27 in Aachen (Aix-la-Chapelle), Germany
1897-1900	Attended the Cathedral School in Aachen
1905	Moved to Berlin
1905-1907	Apprentice in the office of Bruno Paul
1907	Built first house as independent architect
1908-1911	Employed in the office of Peter Behrens
1912	Worked on Kröller house, The Hague, Holland
1912-1914	Independent architect in Berlin
1914-1918	Served in the army
1919-1937	Practiced architecture in Berlin
1921-1925	Director of architectural exhibits for the *November-gruppe*
1925	Founded the *Zehner Ring*
1926-1932	First Vice-President of *Deutscher Werkbund*
1927	Director of Werkbund Exposition, *Weissenhofsiedlung*, Stuttgart
1929	Director of German Section of the International Exposition, Barcelona, Spain
1930-1933	Director of the Bauhaus, Dessau and Berlin
1931	Director of Werkbund Section "The Dwelling," Berlin Building Exposition
1937	First trip to the United States

1938	Emigrated to the United States
1938-1958	Director of Architecture at Armour Institute, Chicago (since 1940, Illinois Institute of Technology)
1938-1969	Private architectural practice in Chicago
1957	Member of the order Pour le Mérite, Germany
1959	Gold Medal of the Royal Institute of British Architects
1960	Gold Medal of the American Institute of Architects
1963	United States Presidential Medal of Freedom
1966	Gold Medal of the BDA Institute of German Architects
1969	Died August 17 in Chicago

(All dates listed are completion dates)

1907   Riehl house, Berlin-Neubabelsberg

1911   Perls house, Berlin-Zehlendorf; later Fuchs house

1912   Project: Kröller house, The Hague, Holland
Project: Bismarck Monument, Bingen on the Rhine, Germany (competition entry)

1913   House on the Heerstrasse, Berlin

1914   Urbig house, Berlin-Neubabelsberg
Project: house for the architect, Werder, Germany, two versions

1919   Project: Kempner house, Berlin

1921   Kempner house, Berlin (destroyed)
Project: Petermann house, Berlin-Neubabelsberg
Project: office building, Friedrichstrasse, Berlin (competition entry)

1922   Project: glass skyscraper
Project: concrete office building
Project: brick country house

1923   Project: concrete country house
Project: Lessing house, Berlin-Neubabelsberg
Project: Eliat house, Nedlitz near Potsdam, Germany

1924   Mosler house, Berlin-Neubabelsberg
Project: traffic tower, Berlin

1925   Municipal housing development, Afrikanischestrasse, Berlin

1926   Monument to Karl Liebknecht and Rosa Luxemburg, Berlin (destroyed)
Wolf house, Guben, Germany

1927   Werkbund Exposition, *Weissenhofsiedlung*, Stuttgart, Germany

Apartment house, *Weissenhofsiedlung*, Stuttgart, Germany
Silk exhibit, *Exposition de la Môde*, Berlin, with Lilly Reich

1928   Addition to Fuchs house, originally Perls house, Berlin-Zehlendorf
Project: remodeling of Alexanderplatz, Berlin (competition entry)
Project: Adam Building, Leipzigerstrasse, Berlin (competition entry)
Project: bank building, Stuttgart, Germany (competition entry)
Hermann Lange house, Krefeld, Germany (badly damaged)
Esters house, Krefeld, Germany (badly damaged)

1929   Project: office building, Friedrichstrasse, Berlin, second scheme (competition entry)
German Pavilion, International Exposition, Barcelona, Spain (demolished)
Electricity Pavilion, International Exposition, Barcelona, Spain (demolished)
Industrial exhibits, International Exposition, Barcelona, Spain, with Lilly Reich

1930   Apartment interior, New York
Tugendhat house, Brno, Czechoslovakia (badly damaged)
Project: Country Club, Krefeld, Germany (competition entry)
Project: war memorial, Berlin (competition entry)
Project: Gericke house, Wannsee, Berlin (competition entry)

1931   House, Berlin Building Exposition, Berlin (demolished)
Apartment for a bachelor, Berlin Building Exposition, Berlin (demolished)
Projects: "court-houses"

1932   Lemcke house, Berlin, Germany

1932-33 Factory buildings and power house for silk industry (*Vereinigte Seidenwebereien A. G.*), Krefeld, Germany

1933 Project: Reichsbank, Berlin (competition entry)

1934 Mining exhibits, *Deutsches Volk, Deutsche Arbeit Exposition*, Berlin
Project: house for the architect, Tyrol, Austria
Project: German Pavilion, International Exposition, Brussels, Belgium (competition entry)
Filling Station (competition entry)

1935 Project: Ulrich Lange house, Krefeld, Germany, two versions
Project: Hubbe house, Magdeburg, Germany

1937 Project: Administration building for the silk industry (*Vereinigte Seidenwebereien A. G.*), Krefeld, Germany

1938 Project: Resor house, Jackson Hole, Wyoming

1939 Project: Illinois Institute of Technology, Chicago, Illinois, preliminary scheme

1940 Project: I.I.T., Chicago, Illinois, final scheme

1942 Project: museum for small city
Project: concert hall

1942-43 Minerals and Metals Research Building, I.I.T., Chicago, Illinois; associate architects: Holabird and Root

1944-46 Engineering Research Building, I.I.T., Chicago, Illinois; associate architects: Holabird and Root
Project: Library and Administration Building, I.I.T., Chicago, Illinois

1945-46 Alumni Memorial Hall, I.I.T., Chicago, Illinois; associate architects: Holabird and Root

1946 Metallurgy and Chemical Engineering Building, I.I.T., Chicago, Illinois; associate architects: Holabird and Root
Chemistry Building, I.I.T., Chicago, Illinois; associate architects: Friedman-Alschuler and Sincere
Project: drive-in restaurant for Joe Cantor, Indianapolis, Indiana

1947 Project: Cantor house, Indianapolis, Indiana
Exhibition of works at The Museum of Modern Art, New York

1948 Project: Students Union, I.I.T.

1949 Promontory Apartments, Chicago, Illinois; associate architects: Pace Associates and Holsman, Holsman, Klekamp and Taylor

1950 Farnsworth House, Plano, Illinois
Institute of Gas Technology, I.I.T.; associate architects: Friedman, Alschuler and Sincere
Boiler Plant, I.I.T.; associate architects: Sargent and Lundy, and Frank J. Kornaker

Central Research Laboratory for Association of American Railroads at I.I.T.; associate architects: Friedman, Alschuler and Sincere
Project: Office building for Indianapolis, Indiana
Project: Caine House, Winnetka, Illinois

1951 860 and 880 Lake Shore Drive Apartments, Chicago, Illinois; associate architects: Pace Associates, and Holsman, Holsman, Klekamp and Taylor
Staircase and interior, The Arts Club of Chicago
Algonquin Apartments, Chicago, Illinois; associate architects: Pace Associates
Project: Steel Frame Prefabricated Row Houses
Project: 50 foot x 50 foot Square House

1952 McCormick House, Elmhurst, Illinois
Chapel, I.I.T.
Mechanics Research Building for Armour Research Foundation of I.I.T.; associate architects: Friedman, Alschuler and Sincere
Project; Architecture and Design Building, I.I.T.
Project: Pi Lambda Phi Fraternity House, Bloomington, Indiana
Project: Berke Office Building, Indianapolis, Indiana

1953 Faculty and Student Apartment Building, I.I.T.; associate architects: Pace Associates
Mechanical Laboratory for Association of American Railroads at I.I.T.; associate architects: Friedman, Alschuler and Sincere
Student Commons Building at I.I.T.; associate architects: Friedman, Alschuler and Sincere
Project: National Theatre of the City of Mannheim, Germany
Project: Convention Hall, Chicago, Illinois

1954 Master plan for The Museum of Fine Arts, Houston, Texas

1955   Cunningham Hall, I.I.T., Chicago, Illinois; associate architects: Pace Associates
Bailey Hall, I.I.T., Chicago, Illinois; associate architects: Pace Associates

1956   Crown Hall (Architecture, City Planning and Design Building), I.I.T., Chicago, Illinois; associate architects: C. F. Murphy Associates
Commonwealth Promenade Apartments, Chicago, Illinois; associate architects: Friedman, Alschuler and Sincere
900 Esplanade Apartments, Chicago, Illinois; associate architects: Friedman, Alschuler and Sincere
Master plan for Lafayette Park (housing project), Detroit, Michigan

1957   Seagram Building, New York, New York, in association with Philip Johnson; associate architects: Kahn and Jacobs
American Association of Railroads Laboratory Building, I.I.T., Chicago, Illinois; associate architects: Friedman, Alschuler and Sincere
Electrical Engineering and Physics Building (Siegel Hall), I.I.T., Chicago, Illinois; associate architects: Pace Associates
Physics-Electronics Research Building, IITRI, Chicago, Illinois; associate architects: Naess and Murphy
Project: U.S. Consulate, São Paulo, Brazil
Project: Quadrangles Apartments, Brooklyn, New York
Project: Bacardi Office Buildings, Santiago de Cuba

1958   Cullinan Hall, The Museum of Fine Arts, Houston, Texas; associate architects: Staub, Rather and Howze
Metals Research Building, IITRI, Chicago, Illinois; associate architects: Holabird and Root
Pavilion Apartments, Lafayette Park, Detroit, Michigan
Town Houses, Lafayette Park, Detroit, Michigan
Project: Battery Park Apartment Development, New York, New York

1959   Project: Seagram Office Building, Chicago, Illinois

1960   Pavilion Apartments and Colonnade Apartments, Colonnade Park, Newark, New Jersey

1961   Bacardi Office Building, Mexico City, Mexico; associate architects: Saenz-Cancio-Martin-Gutierrez
Project: Schaefer Museum, Schweinfurt, Germany

1963   Project: Friedrich Krupp Administration Building, Essen, Germany
Lafayette Towers, Lafayette Park, Detroit, Michigan
Home Federal Savings and Loan Association (renamed, 1974, American Federal Savings and Loan Association), Des Moines, Iowa; associate architects: Smith-Vorhees-Jensen
One Charles Center (office building), Baltimore, Maryland
2400 Lakeview Apartment Building, Chicago, Illinois; associate architects: Greenberg and Finfer

1964   Chicago Federal Center, United States Courthouse and Federal Office Building; joint venture: Schmidt, Garden & Erikson, Mies van der Rohe, C. F. Murphy Associates, and A. Epstein & Sons

1965   Social Service Administration Buildings, The University of Chicago, Chicago, Illinois
Highfield House (apartment building), Baltimore, Maryland
Meredith Memorial Hall, Drake University, Des Moines, Iowa

1966   Project: Church Street South K-4 School, New Haven, Connecticut
Project: Foster City Apartment Buildings, San Mateo, California

1967   Project: The Mansion House Square Tower, London, England; joint venture: William Holford and Partners

1968   New National Gallery, Berlin, Germany
The Science Center, Duquesne University, Pittsburgh, Pennsylvania
Westmount Centre, Montreal, Canada; resident architects: Greenspoon, Freedlander, Plachta & Kryton
Service Station, Imperial Oil, Ltd., Nuns' Island, Montreal, Canada; resident architect: Paul La Pointe
Project: Commerzbank AG (office building and bank), Frankfurt/Main, Germany

1969   High Rise Apartment Building No. 1, Nuns' Island, Montreal, Canada; resident architect: Philip Bobrow

King Broadcasting Studios, Seattle, Washington

Toronto-Dominion Centre, Toronto, Canada; John B. Parkin Associates and Bregman & Hamann, Architects, Mies van der Rohe, Consulting Architect

High Rise Apartment Buildings Nos. 2 and 3, Nuns' Island, Montreal, Canada; resident architect: Edgar Tornay

Project: Northwest Plaza Project, Chicago, Illinois

Project: Dominion Square Project, Montreal Canada

1970   111 East Wacker Drive, Illinois Central Air Rights Development, Chicago, Illinois

1972   District of Columbia Public Library, Washington, D.C.

1973   One IBM Plaza (office building), Chicago, Illinois
Chicago Federal Center, United States Post Office and Federal Office Building; joint venture: Schmidt, Garden & Erikson, Mies van der Rohe, C. F. Murphy Associates, and A. Epstein & Sons
Brown Wing, The Museum of Fine Arts, Houston, Texas

Major structures erected after 1953 are illustrated on the following pages.

Seagram Building, New York. 1957

Toronto-Dominion Centre, Toronto. 1969

Lafayette Park, Detroit. Foreground: Town Houses.
1958. Rear: Lafayette Towers, 1963

Chicago Federal Center, United States Courthouse
and Federal Office Building. 1964

Project: Friedrich Krupp Administration Building, Essen, Germany. 1963. Model

Home Federal Savings and Loan Association (renamed, 1974, American Federal Savings and Loan Association), Des Moines. 1963 Smith-Vorhees-Jensen, Associated

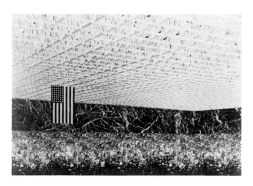

Project: Convention Hall, Chicago. 1953

Crown Hall, I.I.T., Chicago. 1956. C. F. Murphy Associates, Associated

Project: Bacardi Office Building, Santiago de Cuba. 1957. Model

New National Gallery, Berlin, Germany. 1968

Not included are references to newspaper articles. Omitted, too, are some references to books and magazine articles which contain only illustrative material also appearing elsewhere.

The arrangement of Mies van der Rohe's writings is chronological. The rest of the bibliography is arranged alphabetically, under the author's name, or under the title in the case of unsigned articles. Publications of organizations are entered under the name of the organization. All material has been examined by the compiler.

ABBREVIATIONS Ag August, Ap April, Aufl Auflage, D December, F February, hft heft, il illustration(s), Ja January, Je June, Jy July, Mr March, My May, no number, O October, p page(s), por(s) portrait(s), sec section, S September, sup supplementary.

SAMPLE ENTRY for magazine article, DEARSTYNE, HOWARD. Basic teaching of architecture, il Liturgical Arts 12:56-60 My 1944.

EXPLANATION. An article by Howard Dearstyne, entitled "Basic teaching of architecture" accompanied by illustrations will be found in *Liturgical Arts,* volume 12, pages 56 to 60, the May 1944 issue.

Hannah B. Muller

Writings by Mies van der Rohe

1. HOCHHAUSPROJEKT FÜR BAHNHOF FRIEDRICH-STRASSE IN BERLIN. il plan Frühlicht 1:122-4 1922.

2. BÜROHAUS. il G (Berlin) no1:3 Je 1923.
   Reprinted in part in Adolf Behne: Der moderne Zweckbau. p70 München [etc.] Drei Masken Verlag, 1926.

3. BAUKUNST UND ZEITWILLE. Der Querschnitt 4:31-2 1924.

4. INDUSTRIELLES BAUEN. G (Berlin) no3:8, 10 Je 1924.

5. BRIEFE AN *DIE FORM.* Die Form 1:179 1926.
   Comments on exhibition. "Neue amerikanische Architektur" in Berlin.

6. ZUM NEUEN JAHRGANG [AN DR. RIEZLER] Die Form 2hft1:1 1927.

7. RUNDSCHAU: ZUM NEUEN JAHRGANG [AN DR. RIEZLER] Die Form 2hft2:59 1927.

8. [EINLEITUNG] TO ISSUE DEVOTED TO "WERK-BUNDAUSSTELLUNG DIE WOHNUNG STUTT-GART 1927." Die Form 2hft9:257 1927.

9. VORWORT. *In* Deutscher Werkbund, Stuttgart. Bau und Wohnung: die Bauten der Weissenhofsiedlung in Stuttgart errichtet 1927. p76-85 il Stuttgart, F. Wedekind, 1927.

10. ZU MEINEM BLOCK. *In* Deutscher Werkbund, Stuttgart. Bau und Wohnung: die Bauten der Weissenhofsiedlung in Stuttgart errichtet 1927. p76-85 il plan Stuttgart, F. Wedekind, 1927.

11. ZUM THEMA: AUSSTELLUNGEN. Die Form 3hft4:121 1928.

12. ÜBER KUNSTKRITIK. il Das Kunstblatt 14:178 Je 1930.

13. DIE NEUE ZEIT: SCHLUSSWORTE DES REFERATS MIES VAN DER ROHE AUF DER WIENER TAGUNG DES DEUTSCHEN WERKBUNDES. Die Form 5hft15:406 Ag 1 1930.
    Reprinted in Die Form 7hft10:306 O 15 1932.

14 INTRODUCTION. *In* Ludwig Hilberseimer. The new city. pxv Chicago, Theobald, 1944.

15. ONLY THE PATIENT COUNTS. SOME RADICAL IDEAS ON HOSPITAL DESIGN . . . AS TOLD TO MILDRED WHITCOMB. il plan Modern Hospital 64no3:65-7 Mr 1945.

16. A TRIBUTE TO FRANK LLOYD WRIGHT. College Art Journal 6no1:41-2 Autumn 1946.
    ———— See also 27, 27a, 65.
    Reprinted in Emporium, Mr 1948.

Writings about Mies van der Rohe

17. ARCHITEKT LUDWIG MIES: VILLA DES . . . PROF DR. RIEHL IN NEUBABELSBERG. il plan Moderne Bauformen 9:42-8 1910.

18. BEHRENDT, WALTER CURT. Mies van der Rohe. Magazine of Art 32no10:591 O 1939.
    Exhibition, Albright Art Gallery, Buffalo.

19. BEHRENDT, WALTER CURT. Modern building, its nature, problems, and forms. p154-6,170 il New York, Harcourt, Brace, 1937.

20. ——— Der Sieg des neuen Baustils. passim il Stuttgart, F. Wedekind, 1927.

21. ——— Skyscrapers in Germany. il plan Journal of the American Institute of Architects 11:365-70 S 1923.
    Plans of Mies van der Rohe's skyscraper of iron and glass to be erected in Berlin, p367-8.

22. BIER. JUSTUS. Mies van der Rohes Reichspavillon in Barcelona. il plan Die Form 4hft16:423-30 Ag 15 1929.

23. COHEN, WALTER. Haus Lange in Krefeld. il Museum der Gegenwart 1:160-8 1930-1.

24. DEARSTYNE, HOWARD. Basic teaching of architecture. il Liturgical Arts 12:56-60 My 1944.
    Mies van der Rohe at the Illinois Institute of Technology.

25. DEUTSCHER WERKBUND, STUTTGART. Innenräume: Räume und Inneneinrichtungsgegenstände aus der Werkbundausstellung "Die Wohnung," insbesondere aus den Bauten der städtischen Weissenhofsiedlung in Stuttgart. passim il Stuttgart, F. Wedekind, 1928.

26. DOESBURG, THEO VAN. Die neue Architektur und ihre Folgen. il Wasmuths Monatshefte für Baukunst 9:503-18 1925.
    Model for skyscraper, p509.

27. ——— Architectuurvernieuwingen in het Buitenland, Frankrijk, Duitschland, Oostenrijk, Tchecho-Slowakije. il Bouwbedrijf 3no2:74-8 F 1926.
    Includes statement by Mies van der Rohe, p76, reprinted from G no 2.

27a.——— Vernieuwingspogingen der architectuur in Deutschland en Oostenrijk: Peter Behrens, Walter Gropius, Mies van der Rohe [etc.] il Bouwbedrijf 2 no5:197-200 My 1925; no6:225-7 Je 1925.
    Includes statement by Mies van der Rohe, p197, reprinted from G no2.

28. EISLER, MAX. Mies van der Rohe: eine Villa in Brünn. il plan Bau und Werkkunst (Vienna) 8:25-30 1932.

29. EXPOSITION DU "WERKBUND" A STUTTGART: L'HABITATION. il Cahiers d'Art 2:287-92 1927.

30. EXPOSITION INTERNATIONALE DU BATIMENT A BERLIN, 1931; LA MAISON TUGENDHAT A BRÜNN, 1931. Architecture Vivante 9no34:plates 3-8 Winter 1931.
    Illustrations only.

31. F . . . Mies van der Rohe: Wettbewerbsentwurf für ein Verwaltungsgebäude in Stuttgart. il Das Kunstblatt 13:190-1 Je 1929.

32. GENZMER, WALTHER. Der deutsche Reichspavillon auf der Internationalen Ausstellung, Barcelona. il plan Die Baugilde 11:1654-7 1929.

33. GOTFRID, CARL. Hochhäuser. il plan Qualität 3hft5/12:63-6 Ag 1922/Mr 1923.

34. GRAVENKAMP, CURT. Mies van der Rohe: Glashaus in Berlin (Projekt Adam 1928) il Das Kunstblatt 14:111-13 Ap 1930.

35. GROHMANN, WILL. Mies van der Rohe. In Thieme-Becker. Allgemeines Lexikon der beldenden Künstler 24:542 1930.

36. GROPIUS, WALTER. Internationale Architektur. p30,49,69 il München, A, Langen, 1925. (Bauhausbücher. 1)
    Illustrations only.

37. HARBERS, GUIDO. Deutscher Reichspavillon in Barcelona auf der Internationalen Ausstellung 1929. il plan Der Baumeister 27:421-7 1929.

38. ——— Neue Fassadensysteme: Zusammenfassung der Grundsätzlichen. Der Baumeister 27:360-5 1929.
    Discussion of business buildings. Two projects by Mies van der Rohe illustrated, p362.

39. HAUS TUGENDHAT, BRÜNN (TSCHECHOSLOWAKEI). il plan Das Werk 20hft2:42-7 F 1933.

40. HEGEMANN, WERNER. Künstlerische Tagesfragen bei Bau von Einfamilienhäusern . . . Flaches und schräges Dach. il plan Wasmuths Monatshefte für Baukunst 11:120-7 Mr 1927.
    Haus Urbig, Neubabelsberg, Ludwig Mies van der Rohe und Werner von Walthausen, p122-3.

41. HILBERSEIMER, LUDWIG, Groszstadt Architektur. il plan Stuttgart, J. Hoffmann, 1927.

42. ——— Internationale neue Baukunst. p17 Stuttgart, J. Hoffman, 1928.
    Illustrations only of "Entwurf zu einen Bürohaus" and "Wohnhaus in Guben."

43. ——— [Eine Würdigung des Projektes Mies van der Rohe für die Umbauung des Alexanderplatzes] il. plan. Das Neue Berlin hft2:39-41 F 1929.

44. HITCHCOCK, HENRY-RUSSELL. Berlin architectural show, 1931. il Hound & Horn 5no1:94-7 O-D 1931.

45. ———— Modern architecture, romanticism and reintegration. p190-5 passim il New York, Payson & Clarke, 1929.

46 ———— & JOHNSON, PHILIP. The International Style: architecture since 1922. p180-91 passim il New York, W. W. Norton, 1932.

47. HOMES OF TODAY AS EXEMPLIFIED BY THE TUGENDHAT HOUSE WILL BEQUEATH TO THE HOME OF TOMORROW THEIR CHARACTERISTIC OPEN PLAN. il plan House and Garden 74sec2:10-11 N 1938.

48. HORIZONTAL PLANES TO CHART THE COURSE OF EUROPE'S MODERNISM. il House & Garden 61:56-7 Ap 1932.

49. HOTEL PARTICULAR EN BRÜNN. il Viviendas 4:6-11 Mr 1935.

50. JAUMANN, ANTON. Vom künstlerischen Nachwuchs. il plan Innen-Dekoration 21:265-73 1910. House of Professor Riehl.

51. JOHANNES, HEINZ. Neues Bauen in Berlin. p84 il Berlin, Deutscher Kunstverlag, 1931.
Illustrations only of buildings, Afrikanische-strasse, 1926-7.

52. JOHNSON, PHILIP. The Berlin Building Exposition of 1931. il plan Shelter 2no1:17-19, 36-7 Ja 1932.

53. ———— Mies van der Rohe. In New York. Museum of Modern Art. Modern architecture. p111-27 il New York. Museum of Modern Art, W. W. Norton, 1932.
Also issued under title: Modern Architects.
———— See also 46.

54. KORN, ARTHUR. Glas in Bau und als Gebrauchsgegenstand. p161-9 passim il Berlin-Charlottenburg, E. Pollak [1928?]

55. LOTZ, WILHELM Die Halle II auf der Bauaustellung. il plan Die Form 6hft7:241-9 Jy 15 1931.

56. ———— Wettbewerb für ein Bürohaus am Hindenburgplatz in Stuttgart. il Die Form 4hft6:151-3 Mr 15 1929.
Mies van der Rohe, p153.

57. McGRATH, RAYMOND. Looking into glass. il Architectural Review 71:29-30 Ja 1932.

58. ———— Modern synthetic facing materials, il Architects' Journal 74:595-8 N 4 1931.

59. ———— Twentieth-century houses. p166-9 passim il London, Faber & Faber, 1934.

60. METALS AND MINERALS RESEARCH BUILDING, ILLINOIS INSTITUTE OF TECHNOLOGY. il plan Architectural Forum 79:88-90 N 1943.

61. METALS AND MINERALS RESEARCH BUILDING; DRAWINGS FOR THE LIBRARY AND ADMINISTRATION BUILDING, ILLINOIS INSTITUTE OF TECHNOLOGY, DESIGNED BY MIES VAN DER ROHE. il plan Architects' Journal 103:7-15 Ja 3 1946.

61a. Mies van der Rohe, architecte. il plan Architecture d'Aujourd'hui 18no11:36-9 Je 1947.
Includes constructions and plans for the Illinois Institute of Technology.

62. MIES VAN DER ROHE JOINS ARMOUR FACULTY. Pencil Points 19:sup 45 O 1938.

63. MIES VAN DER ROHE TO TEACH IN CHICAGO. Magazine of Art 31:595 O 1938.

64. MONSON, DONALD. Plan for Illinois Technology. il Weekly Bulletin, Michigan Society of Architects 18no46:5 N 14 1944.

65. MUSEUM. MIES VAN DER ROHE, ARCHITECT. il plan Architectural Forum 78:84-5 My 1943.
Project: Explanatory text by Mies van der Rohe.

66. NELSON, GEORGE. Architects of today . . . Van der Rohe, Germany. il plan Pencil Points 16:453-60 S 1935.

67. DIE "NEUE LINIE" IM ALLEINSTEHENDEN EINFAMILIENHAUS. il Der Baumeister 20no11:422-31 N 1931.
Tugendhat house.

67a. NEW YORK. MUSEUM OF MODERN ART. Cubism and abstract art. p156-7, 227 il New York, 1932.

68. OVERSEAERS. por Architectural Forum 67:10 N 1937.
Biographical information.

69. PAULSEN, FRIEDRICH. Der Reichsbank-Wettbewerb. il plan Monatshefte für Baukunst und Städtebau 17:337-44 1933.
Mies van der Rohe, p341-2.

70. PLATZ, GUSTAV ADOLF. Die Baukunst der neuesten Zeit, 2. Aufl. passim il Berlin, Propyläen Verlag, 1930.

71. LE PROBLÈME DES FORMES DES PLACES MONDIALES, ALEXANDERPLATZ, 1928; EXPOSITION DE STUTTGART, 1927. Architecture Vivante 7no25:plates 7-8 Autumn 1929.
Illustrations only.

72. RAWLS, MARION An exhibition of architecture by Miës van der Rohe. il Bulletin of the Art Institute of Chicago 32no7:104 D 1938.

72a. RENAISSANCE SOCIETY, CHICAGO. An exhibition of architecture by Mies van der Rohe. 3p 1947.
Exhibition catalog with foreword by Ulrich Middledorf.

73. RIEZLER, WALTER. Das Haus Tugendhat in Brünn. il plan Die Form 6hft9:321-32 S 15 1931.

74. RUBIO TUDURI, NICOLAS M. Le Pavillon de l'Allemagne à l'Exposition de Barcelone par Mies van der Rohe, il plan Cahiers d'Art 4:408-12 1929.

75. TO ARMOUR. por Architectural Forum 69:sup58 O1938.

76. THIRTEEN HOUSING DEVELOPMENTS. il Architectural Forum 56:261-84 Mr 1932.
Weissenhof Housing Exposition, p276.

77. VON DER DEUTSCHEN BAUAUSSTELLUNG, BERLIN, 1931. il Wasmuths Monatshefte Baukunst & Städtebau 15:241-7 1931.
Mies van der Rohe, p244-5.

78. WEDEPOHL, EDGAR. Die Weissenhof-Siedlung der Werkbundausstellung "Die Wohnung" Stuttgart 1927. il plans Wasmuths Monatshefte für Baukunst 11:391-402 1927.
Mies van der Rohe, p 392.

79. WESTHEIM, PAUL. [Berliner Ehrenmal für die Weltkrieg Gefallenen] il Das Kunstblatt 14:282-3 S 1930.

80. ———— [Das Haus Eduard Fuchs, Zehlendorf] ii Das Kunstblatt 10:106,108 1926.

81. ———— Mies van der Rohe, charaktervoll Bauen. In the author's Helden und Abenteurer. p188-91 il Berlin, Reckendorf, 1931.

82. ———— Mies van der Rohe: Entwicklung eines Architekten. il plan Das Kunstblatt 11:55-62 F 1927.

83. ———— Umgestaltung des Alexanderplatzes. ιl Die Bauwelt 20hft13:312-16 Mr 1929.

84. DER WETTBEWERB DER REICHSBANK. il Deutsche Bauzeitung 67:610 Ag 2 1933.

85. ZERVOS, CHRISTIAN. Mies van der Rohe. il Cahiers d'Art 3:35-8 1928.

86. ———— Projet d'un petit musée d'art moderne. par Mies van der Rohe. il Cahiers d'Art 20-21 424-7 1946.

Addenda

86a. CARPANELLI, FRANCO. Mies van der Rohe. il plan Edilizia Moderna no48:23-36 Je 1952.

87. A CHAPEL. ILLINOIS INSTITUTE OF TECHNOLOGY. il plan Arts and Architecture 70:18-19 Ja 1953.
Includes statement by Mies. Building also discussed in Architectural Record 112:26 D 1952 and in Art News 50:54 O 1951.

88. DAVIES, RICHARD L. "Endless architecture." il Architectural Association Journal 67no756:106-113 N 1951.
Mies, p106-8.

89. FARNSWORTH HOUSE. il plan Architectural Forum 95:156-62 O 1951.
Comments from readers in Architectural Forum 95:70,74,78 D 1951.

90. HITCHCOCK, HENRY-R. The evolution of Wright, Mies and Le Corbusier. il Perspecta no1:8-15 Summer 1952.

91. JOHNSON, PHILIP. Mies van der Rohe. 207p il plan New York, The Museum of Modern Art, 1947.
First edition of this book. Significant reviews appear in Architectural Forum 87:132 N 1947; in Art Bulletin 30:156-7 Je 1948; in Werk 35:sup 142-3 O 1948. Comments on the exhibition appear in Arts and Architecture 64:24-7 D 1947; in Art News 46:20-3, 42-3 S 1947.

92. KESTNER GESELLSCHAFT, HANNOVER. Gropius, Mies van der Rohe. 15p il Hannover, 1951.
Exhibition catalog. Mies, p10-15. Includes reprint of his statement in Der Querschnitt.

93. MIES DESIGNS A NEW LAB FOR RAILROAD RESEARCH. il plan Architectural Record 113:330 F 1953.

94. MIES VAN DER ROHE, LUDWIG. Architecture and Technology. In Three addresses at the Blackstone Hotel, April 17, 1950 on the occasion of the celebration of the addition of the Institute of Design to Illinois Institute of Technology, p2-3 Chicago, 1950.
Reprinted in Interiors 112:116,166 D 1952; in Arts and Architecture 67:30 O 1950; and in Bauen-Wohnen D 1950.

95. MIES VAN DER ROHE. il plan Architectural Forum 97:93-111 N 1952.
Survey of Mies's recent work.

96. MINEHARD, MICHAEL. Mies van der Rohe zum 65. Geburtstag. il plan Neue Stadt 5no2-3:46-51 1951.

97. ROTH, ALFRED. Bemerkungen zu den Wohnhoch-häusern von Mies van der Rohe in Chicago. il plan Werk 38:5-9 Ja 1951.
   The buildings are also discussed and illustrated in Architectural Forum 92:69-78 Ja 1950; Architecture d'Aujourd'hui 20:42-7 S 1950; Bauen-Wohnen no1:1-6 1952; Architectural Forum 98-144 F 1953; Domus no275:1-3 N 1952; and in pamphlet issued by 860 Lake Shore Drive Trust.

98. WACHSMANN, KONRAD. A speech delivered . . . in presentation of honorary degree of engineering, Faculty of Architecture, Technische Hochschule, Karlsruhe, Germany. il Arts and Architecture 68:29,42 Je 1951.

99. WEBER, HUGO. Mies van der Rohe in Chicago. il plan Bauen-Wohnen no9:1-12 D 1950.
   Includes statement by Mies reprinted from 94.

100. ZEVI, BRUNO. Mies van der Rohe e Frank Ll. Wright, poeti dello spazio. il Metron no37:6-18 Jy-Ag 1950.

Addenda II

Listed below are the principal books on Mies van der Rohe published since 1953. A complete bibliography was compiled by J. F. F. Blackwell in 1964 and distributed in a limited, mimeographed edition by the Royal Institute of British Architects, London. The Mies van der Rohe Archive at The Museum of Modern Art is planning the publication of an updated edition of the Blackwell bibliography.

CARTER, PETER. Mies van der Rohe at work. 196p il plan por New York, Praeger, 1974.

DREXLER, ARTHUR. Ludwig Mies van der Rohe. 127p il plan por New York, Braziller, 1960.

GLAESER, LUDWIG. Mies van der Rohe: Drawings in the collection of The Museum of Modern Art. 72p il plan New York, The Museum of Modern Art, 1969.

HILBERSHEIMER, LUDWIG. Mies van de Rohe. 199p il plan Chicago, P. Theobald, 1956.